THE WAY OF LIBERATION

*If you think
by sitting
you can become a buddha . . .*

THE WAY OF LIBERATION

Essays and Lectures

on the

Transformation

of the Self

ALAN WATTS

edited and transcribed by

Mark Watts *and* Rebecca Shropshire

WEATHERHILL

New York & Tokyo

Reproduced on the title page is
a Zen painting by Sengai (1750–1837)
from the collection of the Idemitsu Art Gallery.

First edition, 1983
Third printing, 1985

Published by John Weatherhill, Inc.,
of New York and Tokyo,
with editorial offices at
7–6–13 Roppongi, Minato-ku, Tokyo 106, Japan.

Library of Congress Cataloging in Publication Data:
Watts, Alan, 1915–73.
Essays and lectures on the transformation of the self.
Contents: The way of liberation in Zen Buddhism—
Play and survival—
The relevance of Criental philosophy—[etc.]
1. Philosophy, Oriental—Addresses, essays, lectures.
2. Salvation—Addresses, essays, lectures.
3. Meditation—Addresses, essays, lectures.
I. Watts, Mark. II. Shropshire, Rebecca. III. Title.
B945.W321 1983   128   82–21917
ISBN 0–8348–0181–7

TO
OUR FATHERS
AND
OUR MOTHERS

CONTENTS

PREFACE

THE FOLLOWING chapters hold for the reader a rich selection of literary works and transcribed lectures by the late Alan Watts. They comprise a representative view of his career, from his first essay on Zen Buddhism to his final seminar given only weeks before he died in 1973. Herein, one will find an overview of the formative influences which shaped Watts's philosophy, and which in turn offer the reader a unique insight into the process of realization that, through his works, has given the Western world an unprecedented perspective of Eastern thought.

The opening essay, "The Way of Liberation in Zen Buddhism," was written in 1955, prior to Watts's more extensive work on the subject, *The Way of Zen*. Although *The Way of Zen* contains many of the same concepts as presented in this essay, the essay offers a refreshingly concise and inspired approach to Zen by Watts.

In juxtaposition to the first essay, the subsequent transcription of Watts's last seminar, "Play and Survival," shows how his thought evolved through all that followed. The flowering of his inquiry into Eastern philosophy is perceived as culminating in a playful synthesis of philosophical insight. This interaction is crystallized in the next selection, "The Relevance of Oriental Philosophy," in which Watts discusses the fundamental questions posed by Eastern religions to Westerners of a Christian background.

The next chapter is a lecture transcription, "Suspension of Judgment," in which Watts addresses the inevitable questions and conflicts that arise from the Western man's attempts at self-improvement, and reconciles these with the Eastern concept of *wu wei*, or of letting go, and of non-interference with the way the world is.

In the next chapter, "Chuang-tzu: Wisdom of the Ridiculous," Watts introduces the Chinese philosopher who he feels is most unique in the whole history of philosophy. He presents Chuang-tzu's humorous approach to the purposelessness of existence, and, in doing so, points out that all activity directed toward future goals is meaningless without the continuous, fully embraced realization of the present moment.

How to "live in the present" is delightfully discussed in "The Practice of Meditation," presented here in Watts's own calligraphy and illustrated by one of his drawings of Bodhidharma.

In the developing of this work, I am extremely grateful to Rebecca Shropshire for transcribing and editing the spoken lectures, and to George Ingles for his literary assistance and scholarly advice.

MARK WATTS

Mill Valley, California
September 1982

FOREWORD

To MANY people, the late Alan Watts remains the guru par excellence even though he made no claims to such exalted titles, and rather fashioned himself as a "philosophical entertainer" who merely pointed out the obvious in his own whimsical, yet extremely talented way. His sense of hilarity, his humor and ability to play, his easy laughter, and his claim not to be serious but to always be sincere are truly characteristic of a highly developed degree of consciousness. One is reminded here of the divine in Vedantic philosophy who is always at play, Brahman, totally involved in his *lila,* playing the entire universe; or the Hindu myth of Shiva, who dances the cosmic illusion in his aspect of Nataraja. Watts had a lifelong interest in these themes, and he frequently spoke about them with his usual excellence of interpretation in numerous lectures and prolific writings.

Like all philosophers and mystics who represent the "Perennial Philosophy," Watts's work grew out of a central experience usually referred to as samadhi, satori, cosmic consciousness, or spiritual union with God. In truth, it is this experience that allows a distinction between an enlightened mind, with its clear depth of vision, and the mere abstractions of a groping intellect.

Philosophia Perennis is a phrase which, as far as we know, was first used by the seventeenth-century German philosopher, Leibnitz. At present, it may be used to explain the collective wisdom that grows out of the samadhi experience and that has been universally recorded in the world's great literature, sacred writings, myths, and symbols, from prerecorded time to the present day. Although there have been many attempts to describe this experience of the foremost and highest state of consciousness, it is usually considered futile to attempt any description since this great experience is ineffable.

The Chinese sage Lao-tzu declared in his opening statement to the *Tao Te Ching*, "The Tao that can be explained is not the true Tao," and yet he went on to compose a whole book about it. So too, Shakyamuni Buddha is reported to have said, "What I have to teach cannot be taught," and yet he went on to teach for over forty-five years. In the gospel of St. John we read that when the cynical Pontius Pilate asked Jesus, "What is truth?" there was no reply. Alan Watts was fond of using the Greek word *muein*, which he liked to translate as meaning "mum's the word"—it cannot be spoken. But as is well known, Watts could never be accused of silence, since he has left us over twenty books, countless articles, and an innumerable amount of lectures that fortunately have been recorded on tape. This outpouring of words is indicative of the intellectual's need to verbalize and the poet's need to embellish in order to extract some comprehension from the experience. Thus we have the "Perennial Philosophy."

To the mystic this experience is the criterion of the soteriological, or the confirmation of the redemptive aspect within the entire spectrum of religious experience. Although it can never be imagined, preconceived, or comprehended by the intellect, it seems to occur most frequently through a total and unreserved surrender to the divine. Most often it follows a rock bottom, extremely painful, and intensely desperate state of mind, a strange coincidence of the opposites when abyssmal darkness turns into the most glorious light. Just as the lotus flower grows out of the mud, there is an emergence from a chaotic state to the heights of ecstatic bliss. This brings to mind the occurrence in the life of Ramakrishna as he was about to commit suicide immediately prior to his samadhi in the form of a "revelation of the Divine Mother."

As Alan Watts made vividly clear in one of his finest essays, "This Is It," the individual will interpret this sublime experience within the context of the religious and philosophical milieu of his particular culture, and will express it as a confrontation with or an interior realization of the divine:

> The terms in which a man interprets this experience are naturally drawn from the religious and philosophical ideas of his culture and their differences often conceal its basic identity. As water seeks the course of least resistance, so the emotions clothe themselves in the symbols that lie most readily at hand, and the association is so swift and automatic that the symbol may appear to be the very heart of the experience. Clarity —the disappearance of problems—suggests light, and in moments of such acute clarity there may be a sensation of light penetrating everything. . . . One feels himself taken up and united with a life infinitely other than his own. But as the beating of the heart may be regarded as something that *happens* to you or something that you *do*, depending on the point of view, so another will feel that he has experienced, not

a transcendent God, but his own inmost nature. One will get the sense that his ego or self has expanded to become the entire universe, whereas another will feel that he has lost himself altogether and that what he called his ego was never anything but an abstraction. One will describe himself as infinitely enriched, while another will speak of being brought to such absolute poverty that he owns not even his mind and body, and has not a care in the world.[1]

In the afterglow of this experience, one may realize the cosmic purpose and spiritual siginificance of all life. Total existence becomes sacred. One is overwhelmed with love and humility. All things are affirmed just as they are, and it is felt that everything has always been just right. Although the rapture diminishes in time, the mind retains a sense of certainty and an element that gradually grows into an integral state of being which is eventually expressed in the recipient's everyday life.

Through interior cultivation or by the removal of various obstructions and simply letting "It" flow, some attain the final flowering of the spiritual quest in altruism or loving service. One of the greatest examples we have in the world at the present time is in the life and work of Mother Teresa in Calcutta. However, to these few it does not seem that they attain anything, but rather receive "It" as a gift by grace alone.

But let us give the last word on this to the great historian of religions, Mircea Eliade, quoting from his book, *The Two and the One*, in which he sums up the chapter "Experiences of the Mystic Light":

For all conceptualization is irremediably linked with language, and consequently with culture and history. One can say that the meaning of the supernatural light is directly conveyed to the soul of the man who experiences it—and yet this meaning can only come fully to his consciousness clothed in a preexistent ideology. Here lies the paradox: the meaning of the light is, on the one hand, ultimately a personal discovery and, on the other, each man discovers what he was spiritually and culturally prepared to discover. Yet there remains this fact which seems to us fundamental: whatever his previous ideological conditioning, a meeting with the Light produces a break in the subject's existence, revealing to him—or making clearer than before—the world of the Spirit, of holiness and of freedom, in brief, existence as a divine creation, or the world sanctified by the presence of God.[2]

From a very early age in his life, Watts was fascinated and intensely interested in "all things of the Orient." It is needless to say here that his gifted interpretations of Eastern religion and philosophy are included among the very best. And yet, for some odd reason, there have been both critics and admirers who, having made superficial evaluations of his work, refer to him as a "popularizer" of Zen Buddhism. To the discerning mind, however, it will be apparent that his major contribution is in his interpretation and celebration of the mystical experience. As he himself wrote when he was about halfway through his career:

I saw everything, just as it is now, is IT—is the whole point of there being life and a universe. I saw that when the *Upanishads* said, "That thou art!" or "All this world is Brahman," they meant just exactly what they said. Each thing, each event, each experience in its inescapable nowness and in all its own particular individuality was precisely what it should be, and so much so that it acquired a divine authority and originality. It struck me with the fullest clarity that none of this depended on my seeing it to be so; that was the way things were, whether I understood it or not, and if I did not understand, that was IT too.

Furthermore, I felt that I now understood what Christianity might mean by the love of God—namely, that despite the commonsensical imperfection of things, they were nonetheless loved by God just as they are, and that this loving of them was at the same time the godding of them. This time the vivid sensation of lightness and clarity lasted a full week.

These experiences, reinforced by others that have followed, have been the enlivening force of all my work in writing and in philosophy since that time.[3]

The genius of Alan Watts was in his originality and method—in his ability to remove all obstructions from the mind flow and to simply allow a frolic of words to gush forth in a seemingly magical arrangement of gaiety, wit, and humor with profound meaning and instruction; his gifted use of the English language; his extraordinary memory; and his wide range of interests and learning, which took in not only the history of religious and philosophical thought, but also included the work of such eminent scientists as L. L. Whyte, Gregory Bateson, David Bohm, Joseph Needham, and others, including Korzybski, Sapir, Whorf, and Wittgenstein.

Through his representation of the "Perennial Philosophy," and his synthesis of the views of Vedanta, Mahayana Buddhism, and Taoism, Watts's work has become respected among the less dogmatic and more liberal-minded members of the scientific community. This in turn has opened up more dialogue and communication between Eastern religionists and modern empiricists, which in the course of time should influence even the most elementary educational systems.

In the following lectures, which have been selected and edited by Alan's son, Mark Watts, we have some exemplary talks that Dr. Watts gave between the years 1966 and

1973. Also included is one earlier work that was written in 1955.

One may discover that throughout most of his life Watts possessed an attitude of grand affirmation and joyous participation in all existence. He enjoyed himself under almost any circumstances, had good fortune, and seemed to ride the crest of a wave throughout his entire life.

By familiarizing ourselves with his many writings and lectures, we may find that this same attitude can be awakened in us, and we can join Watts in singing along with Nammalvar:

> He is not: He is.
> Thus it is impossible to speak of Him,
> Who has pierced the earth and the sky
> And become the inner ruler in all.
> He is unaffected by defects.
> He is the abode of bliss.
> Such a person have I attained.[4]

GEORGE INGLES

Berkeley, California
March 1982

THE WAY OF LIBERATION

CHAPTER ONE

THE WAY OF LIBERATION
IN ZEN BUDDHISM

WORDS CAN express no more than a tiny fragment of human knowledge, for what we can say and think is always immeasurably less than what we experience. This is not only because there are no limits to the exhaustive description of an event, as there are no limits to the possible divisions of an inch; it is also because there are experiences which defy the very structure of our language, as water cannot be carried in a sieve. But the intellectual, the man who has a great skill with words, is always in danger of restricting what can be known to what can be described. He is therefore apt to be puzzled and suspicious when anyone tries to use ordinary language to convey an experience which shatters its logic, an experience which words can express only at the cost of losing their meaning. He is suspicious of fuzzy and ill-conceived thinking, and concludes that there is no experience that can correspond to such apparently nonsensical forms of words.

This is particularly true of an idea which crops up repeatedly in the history of philosophy and religion—the idea that the seeming multiplicity of facts, things, and events is in reality One, or, more correctly, beyond duality. This idea is usually intended to convey more than a speculative theory; it is intended to convey the actual experience of unity, which may also be described as the sense that everything that happens or can happen is right and natural in so positive a way that it can even be called divine. To put it in the words of the *Shinjinmei*:

> One is all;
> All is one.
> If only it can be thus,
> Why trouble about being imperfect?

To the logician such an utterance is meaningless, and to the moralist it is plainly subversive. Even the psychologist may wonder whether there can be a state of mind or feeling that such words can faithfully represent. For he may insist that sensations or feelings are recognizable only by their mutual differences, as we know white by contrast with black, and that therefore a sensation of non-difference, of absolute oneness, could never be realized. At most it would be like putting on rose-tinted spectacles. One would at first be aware of rosy clouds by contrast with the memory of white clouds, but in time the contrast would fade, and the all-pervasive hue would vanish from consciousness. Yet the literature of Zen Buddhism does not suggest that the experience of unity or non-duality is recognized only temporarily, by contrast with the former experience of multiplicity. It suggests that it is an abiding experience that by no means fades with familiarity. Our best way of understanding it will be to follow, as best we can, the inner process through which the experience is realized. This will mean, in the first place, treating it from the psychological point of view, to find out whether the words express any psychological reality, let alone any logical sense or moral propriety.

It may be assumed that the starting point is the ordinary man's feeling of conflict between himself and his environment, between his desires and the hard facts of nature, between his own will and the jarring wills of other people. The ordinary man's desire to replace this sense of conflict by a sense of harmony has its parallel in the age-old concern of philosophers and scientists to understand nature in terms of a unity—in the human mind's perennial discontent with dualism. We shall see that this is in many ways a rather unsatisfactory starting point. The problem of telling anyone how to proceed from this point to the experience of unity reminds one of the yokel who was asked the way to an obscure village. He scratched his head for a while and then answered, "Well, sir, I know where it is, but if I were you I wouldn't start from here." But unfortunately this is just where we are.

Let us, then, consider some of the ways in which the Zen masters have handled this problem. There are four ways in particular that seem to deserve special attention, and these may be listed briefly as follows:

1. To answer that all things are in reality One.
2. To answer that all things are in reality Nothing, Void.
3. To answer that all things are perfectly all right and natural just as they are.
4. To say that the answer is the question, or the questioner.

The question itself may assume many different forms, but essentially it is the problem of liberation from conflict, from dualism, from what Buddhism calls the *samsara* or vicious circle of birth-and-death.

1. As an example of the first type of answer, the assertion that all things are in reality One, consider the words of Eka:

The profound truth is the principle of ultimate
identity.
Under delusion the *mani* gem may be called
a broken tile,
But when you enter truly into self-awakening
it is a real pearl.
Ignorance and wisdom are alike without difference.
For you should know that the ten thousand
things are all Suchness (*tathata*).

It is out of pity for those disciples who hold
a dualistic view
That I put words in writing and send this
letter.
Regarding this body and the Buddha as neither
differing nor separate,
Why, then, should we seek for something that
does not need to be added to us?[1]

The implication of this answer is that liberation from the
conflict of dualism does not require any effort to change
anything. One has only to realize that every experience
is identical with the One, the Buddha-nature, or the Tao,
and then the problem will simply vanish. Similarly, when
Joshu asked Nansen, "What is the Tao?" Nansen replied,
"Your ordinary mind is the Tao." "How," asked Joshu,
"can one return into accord with it?" Nansen answered,
"By intending to accord you immediately deviate."[2]

The psychological response to answers of this kind will
be an attempt to feel that every experience, every thought,
sensation, or feeling is the Tao—that somehow the good
is the same as the bad, the pleasant the same as the painful. This may take the form of trying to attach the symbol-
thought "this is the Tao" to each experience as it arises,
though obviously it will be hard to realize much content,
much meaning, in a symbol which applies equally to every

possible experience. Yet as the frustration of not realizing any content arises, it is asserted that this, too, is the Tao—so that any grasp of what the nature of this One that is All may be becomes more and more elusive.

2. Thus another, and perhaps better, way of answering the original question is to assert that all things are in reality No-thing or Void (shunyata), following the doctrine of the *Prajnaparamita-hridaya-sutra*. "Form is precisely the void; the void is precisely form." This answer provokes no attempt to find content or meaning in the term used to represent the One reality. In Buddhism the word shunya or Void implies inconceivability rather than mere nothingness. The psychological response to the assertion that all is One might be described as an attempt to say "Yes" to every experience as it arises, as an attempt to achieve a total acceptance or affirmation of life in all its aspects. Contrariwise, the psychological response suggested by the assertion that all is Void would be an attempt to say "No" to each experience.

This is found also in the Vedanta, where the formula *neti, neti,* "not this, not this," is used to support the understanding that *no* experience is the One reality. In Zen, the word *mu*[3] —no, not, or nothing—is used in a similar way, and is often employed as a *koan*[4] or initiatory problem in meditation for beginners in such a way that at all times and under all circumstances one persists in saying the word "No." Hence the reply of Joshu to the question, "How will it be when I come to you without a single thing?" "Throw it down!"[5]

3. Then there are the answers which seem to imply that nothing has to be done at all, neither saying "Yes" to everything nor "No" to everything. The point here is rather to leave one's experience and one's own mind alone and allow them to be just as they are. Consider the following from Rinzai:

"One can only resolve past karma as the circumstances arise. When it's time to dress, put your clothes on. When you have to walk, then walk. When you have to sit, then sit. Don't have a single thought in your mind about seeking for Buddhahood. How can this be? The ancients say, 'If you desire deliberately to seek the Buddha, your Buddha is just Samsara.' . . . Followers of the Tao, there is no place in Buddhism for using effort. Just be ordinary, without anything special. Relieve your bowels, pass water, put on your clothes, and eat your food. When you're tired, go and lie down. Ignorant people may laugh at me, but the wise will understand. . . . The ancients say, 'To happen to meet a man of Tao upon the road, you must first not be facing the Tao.' Thus it is said that if a person practices the Tao, the Tao will not work."[6]

Similarly, a monk asked Bokuju, "We dress and eat every day, and how do we escape from having to put on clothes and eat food?" The master answered, "We dress; we eat." "I don't understand." "If you don't understand," said the master, "put on your clothes and eat your food."[7] In other incidents the state of non-duality is sometimes represented as beyond the opposites of heat and cold, but when asked to describe this state Zen will say:

> When cold, we gather round the hearth before
> the blazing fire;
> When hot, we sit on the bank of the mountain
> stream in the bamboo grove.[8]

The psychological response here seems to be one of letting one's mind respond to circumstances as it feels inclined, not to quarrel with feeling hot in summer or cold in winter, and—it must also be added—not to quarrel with the feeling that there is some feeling you want to quarrel with! It is as if to say that the way you are actually feeling is the right way to feel, and that the basic conflict with life and oneself arises from trying to change or get rid of one's present feeling. Yet this very desire to feel differently may also be the present feeling which is not to be changed.

4. There is finally the fourth type of answer which turns the question back on itself, or on the questioner himself. Eka said to Bodhidharma, "I have no peace of mind. Please pacify my mind." Bodhidharma replied, "Bring out your mind here before me, and I will pacify it!" "But when I seek my own mind," said Eka, "I cannot find it." "There!" concluded Bodhidharma, "I have pacified your mind!"[9]

Doshin asked Sosan, "What is the method of liberation?" The master replied, "Who binds you?" "No one binds me." "Why then," said the master, "should you seek liberation?"[10] There are other instances where the answer is simply the repetition of the question, or some such reply as "Your question is perfectly clear. Why ask me?"

Replies of this type seem to throw attention back upon the state of mind from which the question arises, as if to say, "If your feelings are troubling you, find out who or what it is that is being troubled." The psychological response is therefore to try to feel what feels and to know what knows—to make an object of the subject. Yet, as Obaku says, "To make the Buddha seek after himself, or to make the mind take hold of itself—this is an impossibility to the end of eternity." According to Ekai, "It is much like looking for an ox when you are riding on it"—or, as one of the poems in the *Zenrin Kushu* puts it, it is

> Like a sword that wounds, but cannot
> wound itself;
> Like an eye that sees, but cannot see
> itself.

In the words of an old Chinese popular saying, "A single hand cannot make a clap." Yet Hakuin always introduced his students to Zen by asking them to hear the sound of one hand clapping!

It is not difficult to see that there is a common pattern underlying all these four types of answers, since all the answers are circular. If all things are the One, then my feeling of conflict between dualities is also the One, as well as my objection to this feeling. If all things are Void, then the thought that this is so is also Void, and I feel as if I am being asked to fall into a hole and pull the hole in after me. If everything that happens is perfectly right and natural just as it is, then the wrong and unnatural is also natural. If I am just to let things happen, what happens when one of these things is precisely my desire to interfere with the course of events? And finally, if the root of the conflict is a lack of self-understanding, how can I understand the self which is trying to understand itself? In short, the root of the problem is the question. If you do not ask the question, the problem will not arise. To put it in another way, the problem of how to escape from conflict is the very conflict one is trying to escape.

If all these answers are not particularly helpful, this is only to say that the human situation is one for which there is no help. Every remedy for suffering is after all like changing one's position on a hard bed, and every advance in the control of our environment makes the environment harder to control. Nevertheless, all this mental circulation does at least seem to produce two rather definite conclusions. The first is that if we do not try to help ourselves, we shall never realize how helpless we are. Only by ceaseless questioning can we begin to realize the limits, and thus the very form, of the human mind. The second is that when we do at last realize the depths of our helplessness, we are at peace. We have given ourselves up for lost, and this is what is meant by losing oneself, or by self-surrender, or self-sacrifice.

Perhaps this will throw some light on the Buddhist doctrine of the Void, on the saying that all is in reality empty or in vain. For if the deepest impulse of my being is to escape from a conflict which is substantially identical with my desire to escape from conflict, if, in other words, the entire structure of myself, my ego, is an attempt to do the impossible, then I am in vain or void to the very core. I am simply an itch which has nothing upon which to scratch itself. Trying to scratch makes the itch worse, but an itch is, by definition, what wants to be scratched.

Zen is therefore trying to communicate a vivid realization of the vicious circularity, the helplessness, and the plain impossibility of the human situation, of that desire for harmony, which is precisely conflict, that desire at our core, which is our very will-to-live. This would be a masochistic discipline of pure self-frustration, were it not for a very curious and seemingly paradoxical consequence. When it is clear beyond all doubt that the itch cannot be scratched, it stops itching by itself. When it is realized that our basic desire is a vicious circle, it stops circling of its own accord. But this happens only when it has become utterly clear and certain that there is no way of *making* it stop.

The attempt to *make* oneself do or not do something implies, of course, an inner, subjective duality—a splitting asunder of the mind's integrity which brings about a paralysis of action. To some extent, then, the statement that all is One and One is all is actually expressing the end of this inner split, and the discovery of the mind's original unity and autonomy. It is not unlike learning the use of a new muscle—when suddenly you move it from inside, or rather, it moves itself, after all efforts to force it from without have been unavailing. This type of experience is vivid enough, but, as we all know, practically impossible to communicate.

It is important to remember that the state of mind out of which this new experience of unity arises is one of total futility. In Zen it is likened to the predicament of a mosquito biting an iron bull, or, as another poem in the *Zenrin Kushu* expresses it:

> To trample upon the Great Void
> The iron bull must sweat.

But how will an iron bull sweat? It is the same question as "How can I escape from conflict?" or "How can I catch hold of myself, or of my own hand?"

Now in the intensity of this complete impasse, in which the radical impotence of the ego is vividly understood, it is suddenly realized that—nevertheless—there is a great process of life still going on. "I stand and I sit; I clothe myself and I eat. . . . The wind blows in the trees, and cars honk in the distance." With my ordinary self reduced to nothing but a completely useless straining I suddenly realize that all this is my real activity—that the activity of my ego has been displaced by the total activity of life, in such a way that the rigid boundary between myself and everything else has completely disappeared. All events whatsoever, whether the raising of my own hand or the chattering of a bird outside, are seen to be happening *shizen*[11] —by themselves or automatically, in the spontaneous as distinct from the mechanical sense of the word.

> The blue mountains are of themselves
> blue mountains;
> The white clouds are of themselves
> white clouds.[12]

And the raising of a hand, the thinking of a thought, or the making of a decision happen in just the same way. It becomes clear that this is, in fact, the way things have always been happening, and that therefore all my efforts to move myself or to control myself have been irrelevant— having had the sole value of proving that it cannot be done. The whole concept of self-control has been misconstrued, since it is as impossible to *make* oneself relax, or *make* oneself do anything, as to open one's mouth by the exclusively mental act of willing it to open. No matter how much the will is strained and thought is concentrated on the idea of opening, the mouth will remain unmoved until it opens itself. It was out of this sense of all events happening by themselves that the poet Ho Koji wrote:

Miraculous power and marvelous activity—
Drawing water and hewing wood![13]

This state of consciousness is by no means a psychological impossibility, even as a more or less continuous feeling. Throughout the course of their lives most people seem to feel more or less continuously the rigid distinction between the ego and its environment. Release from this feeling is like release from a chronic illness, and is followed by a sense of lightness and ease comparable to being relieved of the burden of a huge plaster cast. Naturally the immediate sense of euphoria or ecstasy wears off in the course of time, but the permanent absence of the rigid ego-environment boundary remains as a significant change in the structure of our experience. It is of no consequence that the ecstasy wears off, for the compulsive craving for ecstasy disappears, having formerly existed by way of compensation for the chronic frustration of living in a vicious circle.

To some extent the rigid distinction between ego and environment is equivalent to that between mind and body, or between the voluntary and involuntary neural systems. This is probably the reason why Zen and yoga disciplines pay so much attention to breathing, to watching over the breath (anapanasmriti), since it is in this organic function that we can see most easily the essential identity of voluntary and involuntary action. We cannot help breathing, and yet it seems that breath is under our control; we both breathe and are breathed. For the distinction of the voluntary and the involuntary is valid only within a somewhat limited perspective. Strictly speaking, I will or decide involuntarily. Were it not so, it would always be necessary for me to decide to decide and to decide to decide to decide in an infinite regress. Now the involuntary processes of the body, such as the beating of the heart, do not seem to differ very much in principle from other involuntary actions going on outside the body. Both are, as it were, environmental. When, therefore, the distinction of voluntary and involuntary is transcended within the body, it is also transcended with respect to events outside the body.

When, therefore, it is understood that these ego-environment and voluntary-involuntary distinctions are conventional, and valid only within limited and somewhat arbitrary perspectives, we find ourselves in a kind of experiencing to which such expressions as "One is All and All is One" are quite appropriate. For this one-ness represents the disapearance of a fixed barrier, of a rigid dualism. But it is in no sense a "one-thing-ness"—a type of pantheism or monism asserting that all so-called things are the illusory forms of one homogeneous "stuff." The experience of release from dualism is not to be understood as the sudden disappearance of mountains and trees, houses and people, into a uniform mass of light or transparent voidness.

For this reason the Zen masters have always recognized that "the One" is a somewhat misleading term. In the words of the *Shinjinmei*:

> There are two because there is One,
> Yet cling not to this One. . . .
> In the dharma-world of true Suchness
> There is neither "other" nor "self."
> If you want an immediate answer,
> We can only say "Not two."

Hence the koan question, "When the many are reduced to the One, to what shall the One be reduced?' To this Joshu replied, "When I was in Seishu Province, I made a linen robe weighing seven pounds."[14] Strange as it may sound, it is in this type of language that Zen expresses itself most plainly, for this is a direct language without the least element of symbolism or conceptualism. After all, it is so easy to forget that what is being expressed here is not an idea or an opinion, but an experience. For Zen does not speak from the external standpoint of one who stands outside life and comments upon it. This is a standpoint from which effective understanding is impossible, just as it is impossible to move a muscle by nothing more than verbal commands, however strenuously spoken.

There is, of course, a permanent value in being able, as it were, to stand aside from life and reflect upon it, in being aware of one's own existence, in having what communications engineers would call a psychological feedback system which enables us to criticize and correct our actions. But systems of this kind have their limitations, and a moment's consideration of the analogy of feedback will show where they lie. Probably the most familiar example of feedback is the electrical thermostat which regulates the heating of a house. By setting an upper and a lower limit of desired temperature, a thermometer is so connected that it will switch the heat on when the lower limit is reached, and off when the upper limit is reached. The temperature of the rooms is thus kept within the desired limits. We might say, then, that the thermostat is a kind of sensitive organ which the furnace acquires in order to regulate its own conduct, and that this is a very rudimentary analogy of human self-consciousness.

But having thus constructed a self-regulating furnace, how about constructing a self-regulating thermostat. We are all familiar enough with the vagaries of thermostats, and it might be a fine idea to install a second feedback system to control the first. But then there arises the problem of how far this can go. Followed logically to its limits, it implies an indefinite series of feedbacks controlling feedbacks, which, beyond a certain point, would paralyze the whole system with the confusion of complexity. If this is to be avoided, there must, somewhere at the end of the line, be a thermostat or a source of intelligence whose information and authority is to be trusted, and not subjected to further checks and controls. To this the only alternative is an infinite series of controls, which is absurd, since a point would arrive when the information would never reach the furnace. It might seem that another alternative would be a circular system of control, as when the civilian is controlled by the policeman, who is controlled by the mayor, who is controlled by the civilian. But this works only when each member trusts the one above it, or, to put it in another way, when the system trusts itself—and does not keep on trying to stand outside itself to correct itself.

This gives us a rather vivid picture of the human predicament. Our life consists essentially in action, but we have the power to check action by reflection. Too much reflection inhibits and paralyzes action, but because action is a matter of life or death, how much reflection is necessary? In so far as Zen describes its fundamental attitude as *mushin* or *munen*[15] —no-mind or no-thought—it seems to stand for action as against reflection.

> In walking, just walk. In sitting, just sit.
> Above all, don't wobble.[16]

Joshu's answer to the question about the many and the One was simply unreflective action, unpremeditated speech. "When I was in Seishu Province I made a linen robe weighing seven pounds."

But reflection is also action, and Zen might equally well say: "In acting, just act. In thinking, just think. Above all, don't wobble." In other words, if you are going to reflect or to think, just reflect, but do not reflect about reflecting. And Zen would also agree that reflection about reflection is action, provided that in doing it we do just that, and have no tendency to drift off into the infinite regression of trying always to stand above or outside the level upon which we are acting. In short, Zen is also a liberation from the dualism of thought versus action, for it thinks as it acts—with the same quality of abandon, commitment, or faith. Thus the attitude of *mushin* is by no means an anti-intellectualist exclusion of thinking. It is action upon any level whatsoever, physical or psychic, without trying *at the same moment* to observe and check the action from outside, that is, without wobbling or anxiety.

Needless to say, what is true of the relationship of thinking to action is also true of feeling, since our feelings or emotions about life are as much a type of feedback as our thoughts. Feeling blocks action, and blocks itself as a form of action, when it gets caught in this same tendency to observe or feel itself indefinitely—as, for example, when, in the midst of enjoying myself thoroughly, I examine myself to see if I am getting the utmost out of the occasion. Not content with tasting the food, I am trying also to taste my tongue. Not content with feeling happy, I want to feel myself feeling happy—so as to be sure not to miss anything.

Obviously there is no fixed way of determining the exact point where reflection must turn into action in any given situation, of knowing that we have given the matter enough thought to act without regret. This is always a problem of sensibility, of nice judgment. But the fact remains that however skillfully, however carefully our reflecting is done, its conclusions are always a long way short of certainty. Ultimately, every action is a leap into the dark. The only real certainty that we have about the future is that unknown quantity called death, standing as the final symbol of the fact that our lives are not in our own control. In other words, human life is founded upon an irreducible element of the unknown and the uncontrolled, which is the Buddhist *shunya* or Void and which is the *mushin*, or no-mind, of Zen. But Zen is—beyond this—the realization that I do not merely stand on this unknown, or float upon it in the frail barque of my body: it is the realization that this unknown is myself.

From the standpoint of vision, my own head is an empty space in the midst of experience—an invisible and inconceivable void that is neither dark nor light. This same voidness stands behind each one of our senses—both the external or exteroceptive and the internal or proprioceptive senses. It stands, too, beyond the beginnings of my life, beyond my conception in my mother's womb. It stands at the center of the very nuclear structure of my organism. For when the physicist tries to penetrate this structure he finds that the very act of looking into it obscures what he wants to see. This is an example of the same principle that we have encountered all along—that in trying to look for themselves, the eyes turn away from themselves. This is why it is usual to begin training in Zen with one of the many forms of the koan, "Who are you?"; "Before you had a father and mother, what was your original nature?"; "Who is it that carries this corpse around?"

By such means it is discovered that our "self-nature" (*svabhava*) is "no-nature," that our real mind (*shin*) is "no-mind" (*mushin*). To the extent, then, that we realize that the unknown and the inconceivable is our own original nature, it no longer stands over against us as a threatening object. It is not so much the abyss into which we are falling; it is rather that out of which we act and live, think and feel.

Again, we can see the appropriateness of the language of unity. There is no longer a fixed dualism between reflection and action. More important still, there is no longer a separation of the knower on the one hand and the unknown on the other. Reflection is action, and the knower is the unknown. We can see, too, the appropriateness of such remarks as Ekai's "Act as you will; go on as you feel, without second thought. This is the incomparable Way." For sayings of this kind are not intended to discourage ordinary reflection, judgment, and restraint. Their application is not superficial but profound. That is to say, in the final analysis we have to act and think, live and die, from a source beyond all our knowledge and control. If this is unfortunate, no amount of care and hesitancy, no amount of introspection and searching of our motives, can make any ultimate difference to it. We are therefore compelled to choose between a shuddering paralysis or a leap into action regardless of the ultimate consequences. Superficially speaking, our actions may be right or wrong with respect to relative standards. But our decisions upon this superficial level must be supported by the underlying conviction that whatever we do and whatever happens to us is ultimately right—which is a way of saying that we must enter into it without second thought without the *arrière pensée* of regret, hesitancy, doubt, or self-recrimination. Thus when Ummon was asked, "What is the Tao?" he answered simply, "Walk on!"[17] But to act without second thought is not by any means a mere precept for our imitation. It is actually impossible to realize this kind of action until we have understood that we have no other alternative, until we have realized that we ourselves are the unknown and the uncontrolled.

So far as Zen is concerned, this realization is little more than the first step in a long course of study. For it must be remembered that Zen is a form of Mahayana Buddhism, in which Nirvana—liberation from the vicious circle of Samsara—is not so much the final goal as the beginning of the life of the Bodhisattva. The concern of the Bodhisattva is *upaya* or *hoben*, the application of this realization to every aspect of life for the "liberation of all sentient beings," not only human and animal, but also trees, grass, and the very dust.

In Zen, however, the idea of Samsara as a process of cyclic reincarnation is not taken literally, and thus Zen has its own special meaning for the Bodhisattva's task of delivering all beings from the course of endless birth and death. In one sense, the cycle of birth and death is from moment to moment, and a person may be said to be involved in Samsara to the extent that he identifies himself with an ego continuing through time. It might be said, then, that the real discipline of Zen begins only at the point where the individual has altogether stopped *trying* to improve himself. This appears to be a contradiction because we are almost completely unaccustomed to the idea of effortless effort, of tension without conflict and concentration without strain.

But it is fundamental to Zen that a person who is trying to improve himself, to become something more than he is, is incapable of creative action. In the words of Rinzai, "If you seek deliberately to become a Buddha, your Buddha is just Samsara." Or again, "If a person seeks the Tao, that person loses the Tao."[18]   The reason is simply that the attempt to improve or act upon oneself is a way of locking action in a vicious circle, like trying to bite one's own teeth. Release from this ridiculous predicament is achieved, at the very beginning of Zen discipline, by understanding that "you yourself as you are, are a Buddha." For the object of Zen is not so much to become a Buddha as to act like one. Therefore no progress can be made in the life of the Bodhisattva so long as there is the least anxiety or striving to become more than what one is. Similarly, a person who tries to concentrate upon a certain task with a result in mind will forget the task in thinking about its result.

The irrelevance of self-improvement is expressed in two poems of the *Zenrin Kushu*:

> A long thing is the long body of Buddha;
> A short thing is the short body of Buddha.

> In the landscape of spring there is no
>   measure of worth or value;
> The flowering branches are naturally short
>   and long.

Or the following from Goso:

> If you look for the Buddha, you will not
>   see the Buddha;
> If you seek the Patriarch, you will not see
>   the Patriarch.
> The sweet melon is sweet even through
>   the stem;
> The bitter gourd is bitter even to the roots.[19]

Some Buddhas are short and some are long; some students are beginners, and others are far advanced, but each is "right" just exactly as he is. For if he strives to make himself better, he falls into the vicious circle of egoism. It is perhaps difficult for the Western mind to appreciate that man develops by growth rather than self-improvement, and that neither the body nor the mind grows by stretching itself. As the seed becomes the tree, the short Buddha becomes the long Buddha. It is not a question of improvement, for a tree is not an improved seed, and it is even in perfect accord with nature or Tao that many seeds never become trees. Seeds lead to plants, and plants lead to seeds. There is no question of higher or lower, better or worse, for the process is fulfilled in each moment of its activity.

A philosophy of non-striving or *mui*[20] always raises the problem of incentive, for if people are right or Buddhas just as they are, does not this self-acceptance destroy the creative urge? The answer is that there is nothing truly creative about actions which spring from incentives, for these are not so much free or creative actions as conditioned reactions. True creation is always purposeless, without ulterior motive, which is why it is said that the true artist copies nature in the manner of her operation and understands the real meaning of "art for art's sake." As Kojisei wrote in his *Saikontan*:

"If your true nature has the creative force of Nature itself, wherever you may go, you will see (all things as) fishes leaping and geese flying."

CHAPTER TWO

PLAY AND SURVIVAL

Are They in Necessary Contradiction?

L IVING, it seems to me, is a spontaneous process. The Chinese term for nature is *tzu-jan*, which means that which is so of itself, that which happens. It is very curious that because of our grammar, which we speak in all standard European languages, we are unable to imagine a process which happens of itself. Every verb must have a noun as its subject, a director, and we think nothing is in order unless someone or something orders it—unless there is somebody in charge; thus, the idea of a process which happens of itself and by itself is frightening because there seems to be no authority. In the United States we are in a serious social and political conflict because we think we ought to be living in a republic when the great majority of citizens believe that the universe is a monarchy. You cannot be a loyal citizen of the United States unless you believe that a republic is the best form of government, and yet we are always seeking a monarch, someone else upon whom to push the responsibility. We will not take it ourselves, and we are always complaining that where we are is the result of our past: "My mother and father were neurotic, and therefore they made me neurotic. And their fathers and mothers were neurotic, which made them neurotic" . . . and so it goes back to Adam and Eve. And you remember what happened in the Garden of Eden: God set a trap. He said there was a specific tree, the fruit of which must not be eaten. If he had really not wanted Adam and Eve to eat the fruit, he would not have said anything about it. But by drawing attention to it, it was obvious that they were going to eat it.

So when God saw Adam looking guilty he said, "Adam, hast thou eaten of the fruit of the tree whereof I told thee thou shouldst not eat?", and Adam said, "The woman you gave me, she tempted me and I did eat." Then God looked very severely at Eve and said, "Eve, hast thou eaten of the fruit of the tree whereof I told thee thou shouldst not eat?", and Eve said, "The serpent, he beguiled me!"— passing the buck, you see. So God looked at the serpent, and this is not written in the Bible, but they winked at each other. They had planned long in advance that the universe was not going to be a merely obedient arrangement where I-God-say-you-shall-do-thus-and-so, and you will automatically do it. There would be no fun in that because there would be no surprises. So it is in Hebrew theology that God put into the heart of Adam at the creation a thing called the *Yetzer Ha-ra,* which means "the wayward spirit." Just as when you make a stew and want to put some salt into it, you do not want the whole stew to be salty—just a touch. So God, in creating Adam, put just a touch of wickedness in him so that something surprising and different would happen that God would not be able to prognosticate. Now this is very important. What I am talking about is our sense of identity, our sense of alienation, and the complications we put ourselves into by regarding our survival as a duty.

If you imagine yourself in the position of being God, in

the popular sense of God, the Father Almighty, it means that you are a male chauvinist pig, and that you are in charge of everything. You know all past, you know all futures, you are completely in control of the cosmos, you have absolute power, and you are bored to death. So you say to yourself, "Man, get lost! I want a surprise." And here you are; only you must not admit it. The hallmark of insanity is to know that you are God. It is absolutely taboo, especially in the Christian religion.

Jesus got crucified for knowing it and the Christians said, "Okay, okay, Jesus was God, but let it stop right there. Nobody else." But the Gospel is a revelation to us all of something that the Hindus have known all along, *tat tvam asi*, you are it! If Jesus had lived in India, they would have congratulated him for finding out rather than crucified him. There have been many people in India who knew they were God in disguise. Sri Ramakrishna, Sri Ramana, Krishna, and the Buddha—they all discovered it, because it is not an exclusive claim that I alone am that, but that you all are, and as I look into your eyes I see the universe looking back at me.

So we are in a situation where it is taboo to know that we are God, and we must not admit that we know who we are so as to have the thrill, the sort of self-goosing effect of feeling lost, feeling strange, feeling alone, and of not belonging. We say in popular speech that we come *into* this world, but we do nothing of the kind. We come *out of it.* In the same way as the fruit comes out of the tree, the egg from the chicken, and the baby from the womb, we are symptomatic of the universe. Just as in the retina there are myriads of little nerve endings, we are the nerve endings of the universe. And fascinating things happen. Because there are so many of us the universe is many-sided; thus, its point of view of itself will not be prejudiced. Here we are, and we want to find out what it is that is going on. We look through telescopes to find the farthest-out things, and with microscopes to find the farthest-in things, and the more sophisticated our instruments become, the more the world runs away from us. As our telescopes become more powerful, the universe expands. It is ourselves running away from ourselves.

You know, some years ago we thought we had it. We had found a thing called the atom and that was that. But then whoops! the electron turned up. And then bang! there was a proton. Then when we got past all those there came all kinds of things—mesons, antiparticles, and it got worse and worse. We are a self-observing system which is like the snake, the *ouroboros,* that bites its own tail and endeavors to swallow itself to find out what it is. And this is like the whole quest of "Who Am I?" We are saying, "I would like to see me," but look at your own head. Can you see it? It is not black, and there is not even a blank space behind the eyes—it's just plain nowhere. And thereby hangs the tale. Most of us assume as a matter of common sense that space is nothing, that it's not important and has no energy. But as a matter of fact, space is the basis of existence. How could you have stars without space? Stars shine out of space and something comes out of nothing just in the same way as when you listen, in an unprejudiced way, you hear all sounds coming out of silence. It is amazing. Silence is the origin of sound just as space is the origin of stars, and woman is the origin of man. If you listen and pay close attention to what is, you will discover that there is no past, no future, and no one listening. You cannot hear yourself listening. You live in the eternal now and *you are that.* It is really extremely simple, and that is the way it is.

Now then, I started out by saying that survival, going on living, is a spontaneous process, and love is much the same. The trouble is that when we were children our elders and betters told us that it was our duty to love them. God said: "Thou shalt love the Lord thy God with all thy heart, with all thy soul, with all thy mind, and with all thy strength, and love thy neighbor as thyself." And so our mothers said to us, "You must have a bowel movement after breakfast," "Try to go to sleep," "Take that look off your face," "Stop pouting," "Oh, you're blushing," "Pull yourself together!", and "Pay attention!" And all these are commands, the basic rule of which is as follows: You are required to do that which will be acceptable only if you do it voluntarily. That is the formula. You *must* love me. It is a double bind, and everyone is completely mixed up because of this. The husband says to his wife, "Darling, do you really love me?", and she says, "Well, I'm trying my best to do so." But nobody wants that answer. They want to be told, "I love you so much I could eat you. I can't help loving you, I'm your hopeless victim." So, we are under the compulsion to go on loving just as we are under the compulsion to go on living. We feel we *must* go on, that it is our duty. We are tired of living and scared of dying, but *we must go on*. Why? Well, you say, "I have dependents, I have children, and I have to go on working to support them." But all that does is teach them the same attitude so that they will go dragging along to support their children, who will in turn learn it from them to go dragging along, fighting this thing out.

So I watch with total amazement the goings-on of the world. I see all these people commuting, driving cars like maniacs to get to an office where they are going to make money—for what? So that they can go on doing the same thing, and very few of them enjoy it. Sensible people get paid for playing—that is the art of life. But the whole idea of struggling and beating your brains out in order to go on living is completely ridiculous. Albert Camus, in the beginning of his book *The Myth of Sisyphus*, made this very sensible statement: "The only real philosophical question is whether or not to commit suicide." Think that one over. Must you go on? It would be so much simpler to stop. No problems, nobody around to regret that it was not going on any longer. What is it like—death? To go to sleep and never wake up. Oh, how terrible to be in the dark forever! But it would not be like that. It would not be like being buried alive forever. It would be as if you had never existed at all. Not only that you had never existed, but that nothing at all had ever existed; and that was just the way it was before you were born.

Just as you have an invisible head, your ultimate reality, the ground of your being, is nothing. Shunyata is the Buddhist term for the void—which is space, which is consciousness, which is that in which "we live and move and have our being"—God, the Great Void. Fortunately, there is no way of knowing what it is, because if we *could* know, we would be bored.

There was a great Dutch philosopher by the name of Van Der Leeuw who said, "The mystery of life is not a problem to be solved, but a reality to be experienced." Fortunately, you see, we have in the middle of all consciousness a perpetual question, the perpetual problem that we do not know what it is. Therefore, life remains interesting. We are always trying to find out, but life will not yield the answer. The only way to answer the question "What is reality?" is by classification. Is you is, or is you ain't? Are you male, or are you female? Are you republican or are you democrat? Are you animal, vegetable, mineral, tinker, tailor, soldier, sailor, rich man, poor man, beggar man, thief? We are all put in a class, but what it is that fundamentally *is*, cannot be classified. Nobody knows what it is and you cannot really ask the question in a meaningful way.

There are many philosophical theories about what reality is. Some people say, "Well, reality is material—you know, there's something called *stuff*." And philosophers, because they are always lecturing in front of tables in universities, always bang the table and say, "Now, does this table have reality or doesn't it?" When Dr. Johnson heard about Bishop Berkeley's theory that everything is in fact mental, he disproved it by kicking a stone and saying, "Surely, to every person of common sense this stone is really material and physical." Whereas on the other hand, more subtle thinkers say, "No, there's nothing material, it's all a mental construction. The whole world is a phenomenon of consciousness." In Bishop Berkeley's time they did not know much about neurology. But now we know a great deal more about it and we can state the same position in a much more sophisticated way: it is the structure of your nervous system that determines the world which you see. In other words, in a world of no eyes, the sun would not be light. In a world of no tactile nerve ends, fire would not be hot. In a world of no muscles, rocks would not be heavy, and in a world without soft skin, the rocks would not be hard. It is all relationship, you see. In the old question: when a tree falls in a forest and nobody is listening, does it or does it not make a sound, the answer is perfectly simple. Sound is a relationship between vibrations in the air and the eardrums. If I hit a drum which has no skin on it, no matter how hard I hit it, it will not make a sound. So the air can go on vibrating forever, but if there is no eardrum or auditory nervous system there is no noise. We, by virtue of our physical structure, evoke the world from the vibrations that would otherwise be the void. We are creating the void, but we are also in the world. Our bodies, our nervous systems, are something in the external world. You are in my external world, and I am in your external world. So it is an egg and hen situation—perfectly fascinating. We are, from a very hard-boiled, neurological point of view, evoking the world in which we live, and at the same time we are something which the world is doing. After all, the physicist will explain that you are a buzzing of electronic substances and processes, just like anything else. It is all one jazz, and it is absolutely marvelous because it is aware of itself through you.

The whole of existence is a vibration, and all vibrations

have two basic aspects. We will call one "on" and the other "off." If I am sitting next to a girl in the movies and I feel attracted to her and I put my hand on her knee and I leave it there, she will notice it at first, but if I do not move my hand she will become unaware of it. Then, if instead of just leaving my hand there I start stroking or patting her knee, the sensation goes on and off, on and off, and she realizes that I am paying attention. Everything that is happening to us is going on-off-on-off-on-off-on-off-on-off. Take the sensation of light. The vibration of light is so fast that the retina does not register the off, it retains the impression of the on, and so with our eyes we see things as relatively stable. But if we close our eyes and listen, we hear both the on and the off, especially in the low registers of sound. In the high registers you cannot hear the off, you hear the on. But when you get into the low register you hear the on and the off of vibration. Actually, everything that is physically existing is a throbbing, it is positive and negative electricity. Read the first two paragraphs of the article of electricity in the fourteenth edition of the Encyclopedia Britannica. It is a learned scientific article with all kinds of formulas and technical information, but it starts out with pure metaphysics. "Electricity", says the author, "is an absolute. We do not know anything else that is like it. It is a fundamental. . . ."—and you know he is talking pure theology.

So this is it—everything goes on and off, male and female, yang and yin, now you see it, now you don't. With our nineteenth-century background we have been brought up to think that this energy that goes on and off is inherently stupid, that it is a mechanical thing. Freud called it libido. Others have called it blind energy, and therefore we feel that we as human beings are flukes. A million monkeys working on a million typewriters for a million years might statistically type the Bible. Of course, thereafter, as soon as they got to the end of it they would dissolve again into nonsense. So, we have been brought up to feel that we are flukes, that we are simply accidents. This is alienation, and this is the great problem. It seems to me completely obvious that we are not accidents. Some people say we are nothing but a little bacterium that crawls around on a ball of rock that circles an unimportant star on the outer fringes of a minor galaxy. Why do people say things like that? Because they want to say, "I am a real realistic guy. I am tough. I look at the facts and they are hard facts. The idea that there is somebody up there who cares is for little old ladies and weaklings, and I think this universe is a bunch of crap." That is the message you get from certain people. Always look into a person's philosophy to see what he or she is saying about themself. Your philosophy is your role, the game you put on. I admit that my philosophy is my game that I put on. It is my big act. And if I am going to put on an act, I am going to put on the biggest act I can think of and say, "To hell with all that nonsense, I know very well that I am impermanent, that I am an impermanent manifestation of the which than which there is no whicher." And that is just the way I want it. I am a manisfestation of the root and ground of the universe, which is what all men call God, Atman, or Brahman. And I think it is fun to know that. It is fun to know it not merely as a theory, but as a positive sensation that you can actually feel. Therefore, my function is, if at all possible, to share this feeling so that you will not need anymore psychotherapy, not need anymore gurus, and not need anymore religion—just take off!

There is, however, something called religion for kicks. My favorite church is the Russian Orthodox cathedral in Paris where they really live it up. They have gold, incense, icons, masses of candles, and gorgeous music. The priests come out from the secret sanctuary behind the royal doors which divide the main church from the inner sanctum, and when the doors open, somebody comes out looking like God the Father, dressed in beautiful robes, and it goes on and on and on, and when you get bored you go across the street to a vodka shop where they sell vodka, caviar, and piroshki. Everybody lives it up, and then they go back to church again. That kind of religion is like dancing, it is a joyous expression, and it is not telling God what to do because it is all in old church Slavonic which nobody understands anyway. Everybody is just making great and glorious noises. This is essentially music, and music is essentially play.

Now, herein lies one of the great mysteries of being, because music, like survival, does not really have to happen. Music is a fantasy with no destination. Dancing is the same thing only in motion. When we dance we are not going anywhere except round and round, thus, music and dance are models of the universe. The universe, according to Hindu theories, is going round and round; but according to St. Augustine of Hippo, the universe is going along in a straight line. Now, this was one of the most disastrous ideas that was ever visited upon Western civilization. If time is cyclic, Jesus Christ would have to be crucified again and again. There would not be, therefore, that one perfect and sufficient sacrifice, oblation, and satisfaction for the sins of the whole world. Time had to be a straight line from the creation to the consummation to the last judgment. At that point everybody stopped thinking because they did not know what they were going to do when they got to heaven. They knew what they were going to do in hell. If you look at Jan van Eyck's painting of the Last Judgment in the Metropolitan Museum, it is perfectly clear that everybody in heaven is completely bored. They are sitting there looking like the cat that swallowed the canary. Rows and rows of them with the Lord God Almighty presiding and looking equally bored. But down below there is a bat-winged skull spreading out its ghastly wings, and all-nude bodies writhing and being eaten by snakes and chewing each other. Down below they are having an orgy. But all those stately people up in heaven are destined to stay in church forever, in an obvious state of ultimate boredom.

Also observe Gustav Doré's illustrations of Dante's *Divina Commedia*. He was a magnificent engraver, and while he is on the theme of the *Inferno* he is full of imagination, but when he gets to the *Paradiso* his imagination is shot. All he has is ladies in white nighties trailing in circles through the skies; you know, angels. He has no idea what an angel is! It is a very rare person, indeed, who has a true vision of paradise. And it is extraordinary that our idea of paradise is so weak. Students should write about their idea of heaven to get the imagination going. The point is, we have never admitted that our idea of heaven is a perfectly useless state. What purpose is served by our idea of God? Obviously none at all. Like children when they are little and wise: they make goo-goo noises; the sounds have no meaning, no purpose—and the universe is just like that.

The point is then that life is like music for its own sake. We are living in an eternal now, and when we listen to music we are not listening to the past, we are not listening to the future, we are listening to an expanded present. Just as we have a field of vision that is an expanded width and distance, so the present moment is not just a hairline as the clock indicates. The present moment is a field of experience that is much more than an instant. To hear a melody is to hear the interval between tones. Within the present moment we can hear intervals and see rhythms. Thus, within each moment we can feel a sequence going on.

So, when I speak of the eternal now, please do not confuse it with a split second; it is not the same kind of thing. The eternal now is roomy, easy, and rich, but also frivolous! This reminds me of a wonderful tale about a clergyman of Christ's Church, Oxford, who had terribly bad handwriting. It was so bad that he could not even read it himself. One day he was preaching a sermon and as he started out reading his notes he said: "You who are frivolous, of course, . . . uh, You who are frivolous of course, . . . Ah! You who are followers of Christ!" But do you see the connection? "Consider the lilies of the field how they grow; they toil not, neither do they spin, and yet Solomon in all his glory was not clothed like one of these." This is saying: do not be anxious for the morrow, you who are frivolous, of course.

There is a divine frivolity. The love that moves the sun and other stars is frivolity. Therefore, God might be described as being sincere, but not serious. If a woman who is beautiful and attractive says to me: "I love you", and I say to her, "Are you serious, or are you just playing with me?", that is the wrong response because I hope she will not be serious and that she *will* play with me. So I should say to her, "Are you sincere or are you just toying with me?" You see, playfulness is the very essence of the energy of the universe. It is music. And in my opinion, good music, as written by Bach, has no meaning. Classical music, whether it be of the West, of the Hindus, or of the Chinese, has no meaning other than its own sound. And words, like music, have no meaning. Words are noises that represent and point to something other than themselves. Dollar bills represent wealth, maps represent territory, and words always represent something else. The sound "water" will not make you wet. You cannot drink the noise "water." Therefore, the word is symbolic and points to something other than itself. And yet we say of words that they have meaning. And people get all fouled up because they want life to have meaning as if it were words. Goethe was hung up on this: ". . . all that is mortal is but a symbol." Of what? What do *you* mean? As if you had to have a meaning, as if you were a mere word, as if you were something that could be looked up in a dictionary. You *are* meaning. This is the point: the meaning, the goodie about life is exactly here and now. We are not going anywhere. Look out in the street and you will see people frantically thinking they are going somewhere; that they have important business. They have a far-out look in their eyes and their noses stick out in front. *They are going somewhere, they are on purpose, they have something to achieve.* Here and now, sitting wherever you happen to be, do you realize you do not have to go anywhere? Right where you are is where it is at. That is why the Hindus call the true self of us all the atman, the man where it is at. There is a being in Buddhist iconography called Avalokiteshvara, who is also known as Kannon in Japanese, Kuan-yin in Chinese, and Chenrezigs in Tibetan. These names are usually interpreted as "god(dess) of mercy," and (s)he is represented with 1,000 arms all radiating outward; (s)he is the cosmic millipede, the embodiment of compassion. However, (s)he is not completely a "she." She is hermaphroditic, male/female. Avalokiteshvara means the watchful one, the one who is always caring. The name is easy to remember because as the cockneys say, " 'ave a look it"—"Take a look at it."

Language is simply fascinating. We could go into this and play all kinds of games with words and their music and magic. But now, here is the thing that I am getting at: a culture which excludes frivolity has lost the point of life, and this is where the Chinese communists are in extreme danger. They are the most earnest of people, the most dedicated to survival. The style of life in China and also in Russia is drab because they think that the point of life is to go on living, and so long as you get by, no matter how horrible the food is, how drab your dress, you are getting by. And this is completely missing the point. The mistake is on page 224 of Mao Tse-Tung's red book where he says, "It is essential to have a furrowed brow to think," as if straining the muscles of the forehead has anything to do with clear thinking. This is against Lao-tzu, who is the greatest of all Chinese philosophers, the Father of Wisdom. You cannot make your mind or your nervous system efficient by straining; this is basic to psycho-physical functioning. Mao Tse-Tung makes this mistake and this indicates an excessive seriousness. This is the point I am getting at: life is not worth living if it is compulsive. One might ask why more people do not commit suicide? The vast majority of people could be said not to commit suicide because either they are terrified of it and feel it is an absolute necessity to go on, that is, "while there is life, there is hope" (and that is a terrible motto), or they do not commit suicide simply because they are enjoying the dance. Even if you are not very rich and live in a fairly simple way, nevertheless, the companionship with other people, the sight of the sun and the stars, the rustling of grasses and the sound of water provide your life with its own explanation. As a haiku poem says: "The long night, the sound of the water says what I think."

Herein we have what I am trying to describe as play. Play in Sanskrit is *lila*. *Lila* is the root of our word "lilt," and the universe is called *Vishnu-lila,* the sport or play of Vishnu. Now, when we talk about the play, we also think of the theatre. The theatre is a very curious phenomenon because it is defined by a stage and a proscenium arch. But behind the scenes is a greenroom where the actors dress up. They know who they are in reality before they assume their personas. "Persona" means a mask through which sound passes, *per-sona,* because the masks were worn in the open-air theatre of Graeco-Roman drama. They had megaphonic mouthpieces so that the sound could be projected out-of-doors just as your personality projects your image of yourself, which is not you at all—it is your mask. So, the actors come on, and their strategem is to convince the audience that what is happening on the stage is real. The audience knows by virtue of the proscenium arch, and the fencing off of the stage from the spectators, that what is happening on the stage is not really for real, but the actors are going to act so well that they will have people weeping, laughing, crying, and sitting on the edge of their seats in anxiety. Now, imagine pushing this to a far extreme: the finest actors with the most appreciative audience—and here we are! You see, it is a play. But we take it seriously, and therefore we cannot see through it. We exploit and kill each other, and are mean to each other, but have no real reason whatsoever. Even so, we can understand and see through it, we can know that this whole life is a joke. After all, what is the joker in the deck of cards but the wild card that can play any role. The joker is the symbol of God in the pack. Kings, in ancient times, would always have a jester at court and who was the jester but the man who was crazy. He was a schizophrenic who made unpredictable remarks, and everybody would roar with laughter because he said things out of context. Schizophrenics are in a way liberated because they do not give a damn. A schizophrenic child does not care if he is knocked down by a car— whatever happens, happens. So, the kings had these schizophrenics who were funny people, and they sat at the foot of the king's throne to remind the king not to take himself seriously, as in Richard II:

> Within the hollow crown
> That rounds the mortal temples of a king,
> Keeps Death his court; and there the antic sits,
> Scoffing his state, and grinning at his pomp;
> Allowing him a breath, a little scene
> To monarcharize, be fear'd, and kill with looks;
> Infusing him with self and vain conceit,—
> As if his flesh, which walls about our life,
> Were brass impregnable; and humour'd thus,
> Comes at the last, and with a little pin
> Bores through his castle wall, and—farewell, king!
> [3. 2. 160–70]

Shakespeare is full of this kind of wisdom; *The Tempest* talks of the transcience of life:

Our revels now are ended: these our actors,
As I foretold you, were all spirits, and
Are melted into air, into thin air:
And, like the baseless fabric of this vision,
The cloud-capp'd towers, the gorgeous palaces,
The solemn temples, the great globe itself,
Yea, all which it inherit, shall dissolve,
And, like this insubstantial pageant faded,
Leave not a rack behind: We are such stuff
As dreams are made on, and our little life
Is rounded with a sleep.

[4. 1. 148–58]

The most fantastic things in poetry work on the theme of insubstantiality, of transcience. It is all fading away. We, each one of us, are not a substantial entity, we are like a flame. A flame is a stream of hot gas, like a whirlpool in a river, it is always moving, always changing, and yet it always appears the same. Each one of us is a flowing, and if you resist it, you go crazy. You are like somebody trying to grab water in his hands—the harder you squeeze it, the faster it slips through your fingers. So, the principle of the enjoyment of life is—and this is not a precept, this is not a moralization, this has nothing to do with what you ought, should, et cetera, it is completely practical—do not hang onto it—let it go.

CHAPTER THREE

THE RELEVANCE
OF ORIENTAL PHILOSOPHY

(The following lecture was given before
the members of a Christian theological in-
stitution, so Watts's remarks are directed
primarily along the lines of the relevance
of Asian philosophy to Christianity.)

WESTERN theology has not had a very distinguished
record in promoting the study of other than the
Christian religion, and most study of comparative religion
that has gone on in theological schools has historically
been missionary oriented. This is rather puzzling. The
student of theology has always been encouraged to find out
the weird ideas of the opposing prospects so as to be able
to undermine them. But if you believe in the first place
that yours is the only true religion, is there really any
point in studying any other one? You would very quickly
find reasons for showing the others to be inferior because
that was a foregone conclusion—they had to be. Therefore, in all the arguments about the respective merits of
various religions, the judge and the advocate are the same.
If, for example, Christians get into discussions as to whether Jesus Christ was a more profound and spiritual

character than the Buddha, they arrive at their decision on the basis of a scale of values that are, of course, Christian—making the judge and the advocate the same. I really do marvel at this Christian imperialism because it prevails even among theological liberals, and in practice it reaches its final absurdity in religionless religion—the doctrine that there is no God and Jesus Christ is his only son. It is at this point that we begin to see the anxiety that, even though we do not generally believe in God any more, somehow we have still got to be Christians.

Obviously, the Christian church is a very curious organization that must be understood. The inner meaning of the Church, as it works in fact, is a society of the saved, and a society of the saved necessarily requires a society of the not saved. All social groups with claims to some kind of special status must necessarily create aliens and foreigners. St. Thomas Aquinas let the cat out of the bag one day when he said that the saints in heaven would occasionally peer over the battlements into hell and praise God for the just punishment visited upon evil doers.

Now, I realize I am not being very fair or very kind to modern theology, but there is this strange persistence of insisting that our group is the best group, and I feel that there is in this something peculiarly irreligious, and that furthermore it exhibits a very strange lack of faith. There is a very strong distinction between faith on the one hand, and belief on the other. Belief is, as a matter of fact, quite contrary to faith. Belief is really wishing. It comes from the Anglo-Saxon root *lief*, "to wish," and, as expressed in the Apostles' Creed, belief is a fervent hope, a hope that the universe will turn out to be thus and so. In this sense, therefore, belief precludes the possibility of faith. Faith is openness to truth, to reality, whatever it may turn out to be. "I want to know the truth"—that is the attitude of faith. Most Christians use ideas about the universe and about God as something to hang onto in the spirit of "Rock of Ages cleft for me." Hymnal imagery is full of such rocks: "A mighty fortress is our God," "Unharmed upon the eternal rock, the eternal city stands." There is something very rigid about a rock, but we are finding our rock getting rather worn out in an age where it is becoming more and more obvious that our world is a floating world. Ours is a world floating in space where all positions are relative, and any point may be regarded as the center. Our world does not float *on* anything, and therefore, the religious attitude appropriate to our time is not one of clinging to rocks but of learning how to swim. You know that if you get in the water and have nothing to hold onto, but try to behave as you would on dry land, you will drown. But if, on the other hand, you trust yourself to the water and let go, you will float. And this is exactly the situation of faith. In the New Testament when Jesus began to foretell his own death, his disciples became greatly disturbed because it was written in the Law that the Messiah would not die. To this Jesus replied: "Unless a grain of wheat falls into the earth and dies, it remains alone; but if it dies, it brings forth much fruit."[1] There is also the curious incident after the Resurrection when Mary Magdelene, being so delighted to see the Master again, reached out to grab hold of him, and Jesus said, "Do not cling to me!" On another occasion he said to the disciples: "It is expedient for you that I go away, for if I go not away, the Holy Spirit cannot come to you."[2] Somehow we have reversed all this.

Jesus, it seems to me, was one of those rare and remarkable individuals who had a particular kind of spiritual experience that, in terms of Hebrew theology, he found most difficult to express without blasphemy. He said, "I and the Father are One"; in other words, "I am God." Now, if you are a Hindu, that is a rather natural statement to make; but in our culture, which has Hebrew theology in its background, anyone who says "I am God" is either blasphemous or insane. It is our image of God as "Our Father" that really influences our conception of God, and the image has far more emotional power than any amount of theology or abstraction. It is not like Tillich's decontaminated name for God, "The Ground of Being," nor like Professor Northrop's, "Undifferentiated Aesthetic Continuum." These expressions are not very moving, even though subtle theologians prefer such descriptions. They tell us that when we call God "The Father" we do not have to believe literally that he is a cosmic male parent, and still less that he has a white beard and sits on a golden throne above the stars. No serious theologian ever believed in such a God. But nevertheless, the image of the monotheistic God of the West affects us because it is political. The title "King of Kings and Lord of Lords" is the title of the emperors of ancient Persia. Our image of God is based on the Pharoahs, on the great rulers of the Chaldeans, and on the kings of Persia; it is the image of the political governor and Lord of the Universe who keeps order and who rules it from, metaphorically speaking, above.

Our image of the world in the West is that the world is a construct. Thus, it is very natural for a child to say to his mother, "How was I made?", as if we were somehow put together. This imagery goes back to Genesis, where the story is told of how God created Adam out of a clay figurine by breathing the breath of life into the nostrils of this figurine, and bringing it to life. This reflects the fundamental supposition, that even underlies the development of Western science, that everything has been made, that someone knows how it was made, and that you can find out because behind the universe there is an architect. This could be called "the ceramic model of the universe" because it upholds the basic feeling that there are two things in existence: one is "stuff," or material, and the other is form. Now, material such as clay, by itself, is rather stupid; it has no life in it. So, for matter to assume orderly forms, it requires that an external intelligence be introduced to shape it. Now, with that deeply embedded in our common sense, it is very difficult for people to realize that this image is not necessarily appropriate for a description of the world. Indeed, the entire concept of "stuff" is completely absent from modern physics, which studies the physical universe purely in terms of pattern and structure.

On the other hand, the Hindu model of the universe is a drama. The world is not made, it is acted. And behind every face—human, animal, plant, or mineral—there is the face, or non-face, of the central self, the atman, which is Brahman, the final reality that cannot be defined. Obviously, that which is the center cannot be made an object of knowledge any more than you can bite your own teeth, or lift yourself up by your own bootstraps; it is the basis of what there is, and you are it. The idea being that the nature of reality is a game of hide and seek, which is really the only game there is—now you see it, now you don't.

This Hindu image is one that is particularly disturbing to Christians because in it is the element of a very special theological profanity called "pantheism." Pantheism is the feeling that every part in the drama of life is being played by the Supreme Lord, and this makes Christians think that all the real distinctions between good and evil are obliterated. But practically speaking, that is the biggest bit of nonsense ever uttered. Distinctions between good and evil do not have to be eternal distinctions to be real distinctions, and to say that a distinction that is not eternal is not real is a highly un-Christian thing to say, and certainly a very un-Jewish thing to say. One of the fundamental principles of the Hebrew attitude is that all finite things that have been created by God are good, and therefore a thing does not have to be infinite to be good. Furthermore, to invoke the authority of heaven in matters of moral regulation is like putting a two million volt current through your electric shaver. As the Chinese say "Do not swat a fly on a friend's head with a hatchet". Like all kinds of judicial torture and harsh justice, such ideas bring law into disrespect. Such a fierce God, and such an unbending attitude, results in people disbelieving in God altogether, and, shall we say, "throwing out the baby with the bath water." This is one among many reasons why people today are saying, "God is Dead." It is very inconvenient to have the kind of God who is an authoritarian boss over the world, peering down over your shoulders all the time, knowing your innermost thoughts and judging you. In the so-called "Ages of Faith" people were just as immoral as they are today, so it has never significantly improved anyone's behavior; it is a very uncomfortable feeling, and everyone is happy to be rid of it.

If thou shalt not make any graven image of anything that is in the heavens above, then all these fixed notions of God are idolatrous. The most dangerous and pernicious images are not those made of wood or stone—nobody takes those seriously—they are the images made of imagination, conception, and thought. This is why, in the fundamental approach to the Godhead, both the Hindu and the Buddhist, and for that matter the Taoist, take what is called the negative approach. St. Thomas Aquinas said that to proceed to the knowledge of God, it is necessary to go by the way of remotion—of saying what God is not—since God by his immensity exceeds every conception to which our intellect can attain. When of the Godhead the Hindu says, "All that can truly be said is "*neti, neti*" or "not this, not this," and when the Buddhist uses such a term for the final reality as shunyata, which means voidness or emptiness, textbook after textbook on comparative religion by various theologians complain that this is terrible negativism, or nihilism. But it is nothing of the kind. If, for example, you have a window on which there is a fine painting of the sun, your act of faith in the real sun will be to scrape the painting off so that you can let the real sunlight in. So, in the same way, pictures of God on the windows of the mind need scraping off, otherwise they become idolatrous substitutes for the reality.

Now, I am hoping that this sort of understanding will issue from the "God is Dead" theology, but I am not quite sure whether it is going to. As a matter of fact, there are precedents within the Christian tradition for an intelligent theology such as this, for what I would call "atheism in the name of God." In other words, one completely lets go of clinging to images of God because all such images only get in the way of reality. The highest form of prayer is that in which all concepts of God have been left behind—this is the supreme act of faith. But the moment you insist on the Christian image, you support the Church as a huge, imperialistic, vested-interest organization. After all, if the Church is the Body of Christ, is it not through the breaking of the Body of Christ that life is given to the world? But the Church does not want to be broken up, by Jove, no! It goes around canvassing for new members.

Consider the difference between a physician and a clergyman: the physician wants to get rid of his patients, so he gives them medicine and hopes they will not get hooked on it; the clergyman, on the other hand, is usually forced to make his patients become addicts so that they will continue to pay their dues. The doctor has faith in turnover, he knows that there will always be sick people. The clergy should also have faith in turnover. Clergymen, get rid of your congregations! Say to your people, "You've heard all I have to tell you. Go away. If you want to get together for making celestial whoopee, which is worship, all right; but if you come to church out of a sense of duty, you are not wanted." When I was a chaplain at Northwestern University, I used to tell the students that if they did not want to be at Mass they would only be skeletons at the feast, and it would be much better if they went swimming or stayed in bed because we were going to celebrate the Holy Communion and I meant celebrate!

I think it is a shame that we take religion in such dead earnest. I remember when I was a boy, how wicked I thought it was to laugh in church. We do not realize that, as Chesterton reminded us, the angels fly because they take themselves so lightly. So too, in the *Paradiso,* when Dante heard the song of the angels he said it sounded like the laughter of the universe. They were singing, "Alleluia, Alleluia, Alleluia," which does not mean anything; it is sublime nonsense. So in the same way, there are Hindu and Buddhist texts that are the chants of the buddhas, or the divine beings, and that do not mean anything at all and never did.

The point that I wish to make most strongly is that behind a vital religious life for the West there has to be a faith that is not expressed as ideas and opinions to which you cling in a kind of desperation. Faith is the act of letting go, and that must begin with letting go of God. This is not atheism in the ordinary sense, because atheism in the ordinary sense is fervently *hoping* that there is no God. Thus, faith is letting God go.

Someone once described "Christian Secularism" as the assumption that there is nothing at all to life except a pilgrimage between the maternity ward and the crematorium, and that it is within that span that Christian concern must be exercised because that is all there is. So I am afraid that this is what the "God is Dead" movement might evolve into. It is true that this is pretty much common sense these days. I very much doubt whether most religious people really believe in their religion; it has become implausible. Even Jehovah Witnesses are pretty polite when they come around to the door. If they really believed what they were talking about they would be screaming in the streets. If Catholics believed what they were talking about they would be making an awful fuss—they would be having horrendous television programs that would put pro-football to shame, and they would have full-page ads in the papers about the terrible things that would happen if "you didn't," and more so if "you did." They would also be very serious about it, but nobody is. And so, it has become extremely plausible that this trip between the maternity ward and the crematorium is what there is to life.

You see, we still have going into our common sense the nineteenth-century myth of the universe which succeeded "the ceramic myth" in Western history. I call it "the myth of the fully automatic model," namely, that it is stupid, blind force. Hegel's phrase, "the fortuitous congress of atoms," which is of the same vintage as Freud's libido, is the blind surge of lust at the basis of human pyschology. These men of the nineteenth century were indulging in a put-down attitude of the world, and by making it seem as banal as it possibly could be, they were advertising their own hard-headedness. This was a kind of role playing. On the other hand, if we think about the existence of things and our place in the universe, we might be absolutely amazed to discover ourselves on this "ball of rock" rotating around a spherical fire; it is a very odd situation.

The more I look at things, I cannot get rid of the feeling that existence is quite weird. You see, a philosopher is a sort of intellectual yokel who gawks at things that sensible people take for granted. Sensible people say, "Existence is nothing at all, just go on and do something." So, too, the current movement in philosophy, logical analysis, says you must not even think about existence, it is a meaningless concept. Therefore, philosophy has become the discussion of trivia, and philosophical journals are as satisfactorily dull as any other kind of purely technical inquiry. No good philosopher lies awake at night worrying about the destiny of man and the nature of God because a philosopher today is a practical fellow who goes to the university with his briefcase at nine and leaves at five. He "does" philosophy during the day by discussing whether certain sentences have meaning and, if so, what. However, as William Earle said in a very funny essay, "He would come to work in a white coat if he thought he could get away with it."

The problem is that the philosopher of today has lost his wonder, because wonder, in modern philosophy, is something you must not have; it is like enthusiasm in eighteenth-century England—it is very bad form. I wonder about the universe, but it is not a question that I wonder about, it is a feeling that I have. I do not even know what question to ask! What would you ask? Imagine if you had an interview with God and were allowed to ask one question. What would it be? If you do not rush to answer, you will soon find that you have no idea what to ask. I simply cannot formulate the question that contains my wonder. The moment my mouth opens to utter it, I suddenly find I am talking nonsense. Yet this should not prevent wonder from being the foundation of philosophy. As Aristotle said, "Wonder is the beginning of philosophy." To the philosopher, existence seems very strange, and even more so when he realizes that we are all embraced within a neurological contraption that is able to center itself in the midst of an incredible expanse of galaxies and then start measuring the whole thing. Existence is relationship, and we are smack in the middle of it.

Obviously, there is a place in life for a religious attitude in the sense of awe, of astonishment at existence. And this is also a basis of respect for existence—which is something we do not have very much of in this culture, even though we call it materialistic. A materialist is a person who loves material, but in our culture today we are bent on the total destruction of material and its conversion into junk and poisonous gas as quickly as possible. Ours is not a materialistic culture because it has no respect for material. And respect is, in turn, based on wonder—on feeling the marvel of just an ordinary pebble in your fingers.

So I am afraid that the "God is Dead" theology will sort of drift off into secular do-goodery in the name of Jesus. And this, I think, is where we can be strongly revivified and stimulated by the introduction into our spiritual life of certain things that are Oriental. Now, it must be understood that the crux of the Hindu and Buddhist disciplines is an experience; it is not a theory, nor is it a belief. If we say that a religion is a combination of creed, code, and cult—as is true of Judaism, Islam, and Christianity—then Buddhism is not. A creed is a revelation, a revealed symbolism of what the universe is about, and you are commanded to believe in it on divine authority; a code is the revealed will of God for man, which you are commanded to obey; and a cult is the divinely revealed form of worship that you must practice. The Ten Commandments must be obeyed because God is boss. He is the ruler, King of Kings and Lord of Lords. But the discipline of yoga in Hinduism, or in the various forms of Buddhist meditation, do not require you to believe anything, and they contain no commandments. They do indeed have precepts, but they are really vows that you undertake on your own responsibility, not as an obedience to someone. They are experimental techniques for changing consciousness, and the thing that they are mainly concerned with is helping human beings to get rid of the hallucination that each one of us is a skin-encapsulated ego—a little man inside our head located between the ears and behind the eyes who is the source of conscious attention and voluntary behavior. Most people do not really think that they are anything but that, and that the body is a thing that you have. "Mommie, who would I have been if my father had been someone else?", as though your parents give you the body and you pop the soul into it at some point—conception or parturition, nobody could ever decide.

This attitude, that we are something in a body, is one that lingers with us. We are taught to experience the beating of the heart as something that happens to us, whereas talking or walking is something that we do. But, do you not beat your heart? Language will not allow you to think that; it is not customary. How do you even think? How do you manage to be conscious? Do you know? How do you open and close your hand? If you are a physiologist, you may be able to say, but that does not help you to open and close your hand any better than I do. I know how to do it, but I cannot put it into words. In the same way, the Hindu god knows how he creates this whole universe because he does it, but he could not explain it. He might as well try to drink the Pacific Ocean with a fork. So when a Hindu gets enlightened and he recovers from the hallucination of being a skin-encapsulated ego, he finds out that central to his own self is the eternal self of the universe, and if you go up to him and say, "How do you do all this?", he is apt to say, "Well, just like you open and close your hand."

Whenever questioners would go to Sri Ramana, the great Hindu sage who died a few years ago, they would say to him, "Master, was I living before in a previous incarnation, and if so, who was I?", and he would say to them, "Who is asking the question? Who are you?" What a spiritual teacher in both Hinduism and Buddhism does to awaken you, to get you over the hallucination of being the skin-encapsulated ego, is to bug you in a certain way. He has a funny look in his eyes as if to say, "Come off it, Shiva, I know what you are up to, I know what you are doing." And you say, "What, me?" So he looks at you in a funny way, until finally you get the feeling that he sees all the way through you; and that all your selfishness and evil, nasty thoughts are transparent to his gaze. Then you have to try and alter them. He suggests that you practice the control of the mind, that you become desireless, and that you give up selfish desires so as to be a skin-encapsulated *self*. Then you may have some success in quieting your mind and in concentrating. But after that, he will throw a curve at you, which is: But are you not still desiring not to desire? Why are you trying to be unselfish? Well, the answer is, "I want to be on the side of the big battalions. I think it is going to pay off better to be unselfish than to be selfish." Luther saw that, and St. Augustine saw it also. But there it is—he has begun to make you see the unreality and the hallucinatory quality of a separate self. Such a self is merely conventional reality, in the same sense as lines of latitude and longitude and the measurements of the clock; which is why one of the means of maya, illusion, is measurement. Things are measurements; they are units of thought, like inches are units of measurement. There are no *things* in physical nature. How many things is a thing? However many you want. A "thing" is a "think," a unit of thought; it is as much reality as you can catch hold of in one idea.

So when this realization of the hallucination of the separate self comes about, it comes about through discovering that your alleged separate self cannot do anything—it cannot improve itself either by doing something about it, or by doing nothing about it, and both ways are based on illusion. You see, this is what you have to do to get people out of hallucinations—you make them act consistently on the suppositions of their hallucinations. The guru, whether Hindu or Buddhist, performs a *reductio ad absurdum* on the premise of the skin-encapsulated ego. So, what happens then? You might imagine from garbled accounts of Eastern mysticism that one thereupon disappears into an infinite sea of faintly mauve jello, and that you become so lost to the world, and so entranced, that you forget your name, address, telephone number, and function in life. But nothing of the kind happens. The state of mystical illumination, although it may in its sudden onset be accompanied by a sensation of tremendous luminance and transparency, when you get used to it, it is just like everyday life. Here are the people that you formerly thought were separate individuals, and here is the "you" whom you formerly thought was merely confronting these other people. When the great Dr. D. T. Suzuki was asked, "What is it like to be enlightened?" he said, "It is just like ordinary, everyday experience, except about two inches off the ground." You see, what is altered is not the way your senses perceive; what is altered is the way you think about it—your definitions of what you see, and your evaluation of it. When you do not cling to the world, and when you no longer have a hostile attitude toward it, you know the world is you. Taken from the point of view of biology, the behavior of a living organism cannot possibly be described without simultaneously describing the behavior of the environment. To describe organisms in environments is to describe a unified field of behavior called an "organism-environment." The environment does not push the organism around and the organism does not push the environment around. They are two aspects, or poles, of the same process.

This attitude toward nature—seeing the fundamental unity of the self that manifests it all—is not an attitude that, as missionaries are apt to suppose, denies the value of differentiation. You must understand the principle of what are called identical differences. Take a coin. The head side is a different side from the tail side, and yet the two are inseparable. Take the operation of buying and selling. Selling is a separate operation from buying, but you cannot buy anything unless somebody sells something at the same time, and vice versa. This is what is meant by the underlying unity of opposites, what is called Advaita, or nonduality, in Hinduism; and what the Chinese mean when they use the word *tao* to designate the way of operation of the positive and negative principles, the yang and the yin. It is not a unity that annihilates differences, but a unity that is manifested by the very differentiations that we perceive. It is all polar, like the two poles of one magnet.

So when we say that Oriental monism is a point of view toward life that merges everything into a kind of sickening goo, this is terribly unfair; it just is not so. If you argue that this sort of doctrine, in which everybody is really the Godhead, destroys the possibility of love between individuals because you have to be definitively "other" in order to love, otherwise it is all self-love, then that argument collapses in view of the doctrine of the Trinity. If the three persons are one God, then they cannot love each other by the same argument. Hinduism simply uses the idea that is in the Christian Trinity, only it uses the idea of a multi-trinity. Instead of a three-in-one, it is a one-in-All.

Of course, the thorn in the flesh, when approaching a doctrine that seems to be monistic or pantheistic, is always: what about evil? Are we to make the ground of being responsible for evil? No, we do not want to do that because we want to keep God's skirts clean. In spite of the fact that our Hebrew Bible says: "I am the Lord, and there is none else; I form the light and create darkness; I make peace, and create evil. I the Lord do all these things."[3]

Who is it that sits at the left hand of God? (We know who sits at the right hand.) All word about the one who sits on the left is hushed up because that is the side on which the district attorney sits. Of course, in the Book of Job, it is Satan who is the district attorney in the court of heaven. He is the prosecutor and faithful servant of the court. The whole problem is that it would be very bad indeed if God were the author of evil, and we were his victims. That is to say, if we keep the model of the king of the universe in which the creatures are all subjects of the king, then a God who is responsible for evil is being very unkind to the people. But in the Hindu theory, God is not another person. There are no victims of God. He is never anything but His own victim. You are responsible. If you want to stay in the state of illusion, stay in it. But you can always wake up.

ORIENTAL PHILOSOPHY *53*

CHAPTER FOUR

SUSPENSION OF JUDGMENT

The Tangle of Transformation

HUMAN beings have for a long time been concerned about transforming their minds. But may I ask: is there any way in which one's mind *can* be transformed, or is it simply a process that is nothing more than a vicious circle? In so many people's minds there is an urgent feeling that "I must improve me," and this is critically important. In the very idea that "I must improve me" there is the obvious difficulty that if I am in need of improvement, the "I" who is going to do the improving is the one who needs to be improved; and there, immediately, we have a vicious circle.

If I may put this in theological terms: how does man follow the will of God if the will of man is perverse? Theologians say you cannot follow the will of God without having divine grace. How, then, do you get grace? Why is grace given to some and not to others? If I cannot follow the will of God by my own effort because my will is selfish, how will my will, which is selfish, be transformed into an unselfish will? If I cannot do it, then grace must do it. If grace has not already done it, why not? Because I did not accept it? But by definition I had no power to accept it because my will was selfish. Must I then become a Calvinist and say that only those people who are predestined to receive grace will be able to live the good life? Following this line of questioning, we come to the inadmissable position that people who lead evil lives do not get grace because they are not predestined to it out of the infinite wisdom of the Godhead, and that God himself must then be held responsible for their evil deeds. This is a nice little tangle.

In the language of Oriental philosophy, the problem of transformation sounds something like this: the Buddha said that wisdom can come only from the abandonment of selfish craving, or desire. One who abandons that desire attains nirvana, which means supreme peace and liberation. In Sanskrit, nirvana means to blow out, to exhale the breath. Its opposite, desire, is to breathe in. Now, if you breathe in and hold it, you lose your breath; but if you breathe out it comes back to you. So the point is: if you want life, do not cling to it, let it go. Still there is the problem that if I desire not to desire, is that not already desire? How can I desire not to desire? How can I surrender myself when myself is precisely an urge to hold on, to cling, to cling to life, to continue to survive? I can see rationally that by clinging to myself I may strangle myself, and so I may chose to be like a person who has a bad habit as a result of which he is committing suicide because the means of death are so sweet.

I am sure you have observed how people who get interested in improving themselves behave. They usually shop around quite a bit. They try out psychoanalysis, psychodrama, encounter groups, yoga, Scientology, Christian Science, Roman Catholicism, Zen Buddhism, or Tibetan Buddhism, and whenever they have hold of one of these things it is the absolute rage—"Man, you've got to dig this." But we notice that nothing fundamentally different happens. It is always the same old guy going around with a new bag of tricks. He does not really change, only his ways of trying to change do.

One of the basic forms in which you notice that there is no change is the nature of what I will call the self-improvement game. This is a game we are all playing from one point of view or another. I could ask: what are you looking for? Would it be too presumptuous of me to say that you are looking for help? That you would like to hear someone who has something of relevance to say to you as a member of a world which is running into the most intense difficulty? Our world is beset by a complex of problems, any one of which is bad enough; but when you add together all the great political, social, and ecological problems with which we are faced, it is appalling. One might naturally say that the reason why we are in such a mess is not simply that we have wrong systems for doing things, whether they be technological, political, or religious, but that we have the wrong people. The systems may be all right, but they are in the wrong hands, because we are all in various ways self-seeking, lacking in wisdom, lacking in courage, afraid of death, afraid of pain, unwilling really to cooperate with others, and unwilling to be open to others. So we all think: "It's really *me* that's wrong. If only I could be the right person. And is this man going to tell me something that will make me be a more creative and cooperative member of the human race? I sincerely would like to improve."

So I imagine that many of you hope that I will tell you something to make you better, better in whatever sense you want to use that word—to feel better, to be morally better, to be a better citizen, or to have a higher state of consciousness. Perhaps some of you have mystical ambitions and want to transcend your feeling of egocentricity, of being an isolated center of consciousness inside a bag of skin; perhaps you would like to experience cosmic consciousness and to feel that you yourself are basically identical with the infinite energy of this universe. Mystics have often had that experience, and you would like it; and you would also appreciate getting from me some advice as to how that might come about. You may say, "I need some help in this process, and I am going to find someone else to help me." You may chose a therapist, or a clergyman, or even a guru—any kind of person who teaches a technique of self-improvement. But how will you know whether this person is able to teach you? How can you judge, for example, whether a psychotherapist is effective or just a charlatan? How can you judge whether a guru is himself spiritually wise or merely a good chatterbox? Well, of course you ask your friends, or you ask his other students or patients, and, of course, they are all enthusiastic. You have to be enthusiastic when you have bought something expensive. If you have bought an automobile that has turned out to be a lemon, it is very difficult to admit that it is a lemon and that you have been fooled. And it is the same when you buy a religion or an expensive operation. But what people do not sufficiently realize is that when you picked an authority, whether it is a psychotherapeutic or a religious one, *you* chose it. In other words, that this fellow, or this book, or this system, is the right one is *your* opinion. If you are saying to this other person, or other source: "I think you are the authority"—that is your opinion. And how are you competent to judge? You cannot really judge whether an authority is sound unless you yourself are. Otherwise, you might just be fooled. You may say, "I believe that the Bible is the word of God"—all right, that is your opinion. I know the Bible says it is the word of God, but it is your opinion that the Bible is telling the truth. The Church says that the Bible is the word of God, but it is your opinion that the Church is right. You cannot escape from this situation—it is your opinion.

At this point, it might be obvious to you that when selecting an authority who will help you to improve yourself it is like hiring the police out of *your* tax money and putting them in charge of seeing that you obey the law. This seems pretty silly—can we not take care of ourselves? Is this the land of the free and the home of the brave, or not? Nobody seems to want to be in charge of themselves because they feel they cannot do it. As St. Paul said, "To will is present with me. But how to do good I find not, for the good that I would, I do not, and the evil that I would not, that I do." Here at once we are in difficulty because trying to improve ourselves is like trying to lift ourselves up into the air by tugging at our own bootstraps. It just cannot be done! There are, however, all sorts of ways in which religious people try to explain that it *can* be done. But you cannot do the job by yourself because the improving "you" is the one that needs to be improved. Therefore, you have to say, "God help me." Of course, that God exists is your opinion; that God will answer your prayer is your opinion; and your idea of God is *your* idea of God. If you bought someone else's script—you bought it! Maybe your mother and father talked to you about God in a very impressive way, but basically, you bought their idea. You may be a father yourself. I am a grandfather now. I have five grandchildren, and I know I am as stupid as my own grandfather must have been. I sit in the position from which they look at me and think, "Oh, wow! There's an important man!" But I know I am just like anyone else. So I hope my children are not believing things on my authority, because it is always *their* authority. If I look impressive and make big noises at them, they have just been taken in.

So let us suppose there is God, and that there is available grace—the divine power that gives the human being a rope to climb upon instead of just pulling at his own bootstraps. All right, you want grace. A theologian will tell you, "Yes, God gives His grace freely. He gives it to all because He loves all. It is here like the air, all you have to do is receive it." Or, a more orthodox, perhaps Catholic, Christian will say, "All you have to do is be baptized and take the holy sacrament of the altar, the bread and wine, the body and blood of Christ. There is grace right there. It is given by these simple physical means so that it is very easily available." Well, a lot of people have been baptized, but it does not always take. People fall from grace. Why do they? You see, we are still talking about the same old problem but we have put it one step up. "How can I improve myself?", was the first problem, and the second problem is, "How can I accept graee?", but they are both the same problem because in each case you have got to make a move that will put yourself out of your own control into the control of a "better." And if you do not believe in the Christian kind of a God you can believe in the Hindu kind of a God who is your inner self. You have a lower self that you call your ego—that is that little scoundrelly fellow that is always out for "me." But behind the ego there is the atman, the inner self, or the inward light, as the Quakers call it; it is the real self, the spirit that is substantially identical with God. So you have to meditate in such a way that you identify with your higher self.

But how do you do that? Well, you start by watching all of your thoughts very carefully. You watch your feelings, you watch your emotions, and you begin to build up a sense of separation between the watcher and what is watched. In this way, you are no longer carried away by your own stream of consciousness. You remain the witness, impassively, impartially suspending judgment and watching it all go on.

Now, this seems to be something like progress—at least you are taking an objective view of what is happening, and you are beginning to be in a position to control it. But just wait a minute! Who is this self behind the self, the watching self? Can you watch *that* one? It is interesting if you do because you find out, of course, that the watching self, or the observing self, behind all your thoughts and feelings is itself a thought. That is to say, when the police enter a house in which there are thieves, the thieves go up from the ground floor to the first floor. When the police arrive on the first floor, the thieves have gone up to the second, and so on to the third and finally out onto the roof. Just so, when the ego is about to be unmasked, it immediately identifies with the higher self. It goes up a level, because the religious game version is simply a refined and high-brow version of the ordinary game: "How can I outwit me?" So if I find, for example, that in the quest for pleasure, the ordinary pleasures of the world—food, sex, power, possessions—become a drag and I think, "No, it is not that," and then I go in for the arts, literature, poetry, and music, and I absorb myself in those pleasures, then after awhile I find that they are not the answer either. So then I go in for psychoanalysis, and I find out that is not the answer, and then I turn to religion, but I'm still seeking what I was seeking when I wanted candy bars! I want to get that goodie. Only I see now that it is not going to be a material goodie because all material goodies fall apart; but maybe there is a spiritual goodie that will not. Still, the spiritual quest is no different than the quest for the candy bar. Same old story, only you have refined the candy bar and made it abstract and holy and blessed and so on. So it is with the higher self. The higher self is your same old ego, but you sure hope it is eternal, indestructable, and all-wise.

The great problem is how to get this higher self working. How does it make any difference to what you do and what you think? I know all kinds of people who have this higher self going. They practice their yoga, and they are just like ordinary people, sometimes a little worse. You see, they too can fool themselves. They can say, "My point of view in religion is very liberal. I believe that all religions have divine revelations in them, so I do not understand the way you people fight about it." Others say, "Well, God has given the spirit through all the traditions but *our's* is the most refined and mature." Then somebody else comes along and says, "Well, as I said, they are all equally revelations of the divine and in seeing this, of course, I am much more tolerant than you are." You see how this game is going to work?

Suppose I take this position: Let us say you regard me as some kind of a guru. Well, you know how gurus hate each other and are always putting each other down. But I could say, "Well, I do not put other gurus down," and that outwits them all. You see, we are always doing this. We are always finding a way to be one up, and by the most incredibly subtle means. You may say, "I realize that I am always doing that, now tell me, how do I not do that?" And I will say, "Why do you want to know?" "Well, I would be better that way", you would say. "Yes, but why do you want to be better?" You see, the reason why you want to be better is the reason why you are not—it is because you *want* to be, and do not realize that you already are. "The road to hell is paved with good intentions" because the do-gooders in the world, whether they are doing good for others or doing good for themselves, are troublemakers on the basis of: "Kindly let me help you or you will drown," said the monkey putting the fish safely up in a tree.

We European-Americans have been on the rampage for the last one hundred years or more to improve the world. We have given the benefits of our culture—our religion and our technology—to everyone (except perhaps the Australian aborigines). We have insisted that they receive the benefits of our culture and even our political style: "You better be democratic, or we will shoot you!" And having conferred these blessings all over the place we wonder why the rest of the world dislikes us. Sometimes doing good to others, and even doing good to oneself, is amazingly destructive. And it is also full of conceit. How do you know what is good for other people? How do you know what is good for you? If you say that you want to improve, then you ought to know what is good for you, but obviously you do not, because if you did you would already be improved.

So we do not know. It is like the problem that geneticists are faced with today. I went to a meeting of geneticists not so long ago where they gathered in a group of philosophers and theologians and said, "Now look here, we need help. We are now on the verge of figuring out how to breed any kind of human character we might want to have. We could give you saints, philosophers, scientists, great politicians, anything you want. Just tell us. What kind of human beings ought we to breed?" So I said, "How will those of us who are genetically unregenerate make up our minds what genetically generate people might be? I am very much afraid that our selection of virtues may not work. It may be like this new kind of high-yield grain that is becoming ecologically destructive. When we interfere with the processes of nature and breed efficient plants and animals, there is always some way in which we have to pay for it. And I can well see that eugenically produced human beings might be dreadful." Do you not realize that we could have a plague of virtuous people? I mean, any animal considered by itself is virtuous, doing its own thing, but in crowds they are awful. Like a crowd of ants or locusts on the rampage, I could imagine a perfectly pestiferous mass of a million saints. So I said to the geneticists, "Just be sure that a vast variety of human beings are maintained. Please do not breed us down to a few excellent types—excellent for what? We never know how circumstances are going to change, or how our need for different kinds of people might change. At one time we may need very individualistic and aggressive people, at another time we may need very cooperative, team-working people, and at another time we may need people who are full of interest in the dexterous manipulation of the external world. Still, at another time we may need people who can explore their own psychology and are introspective. There is no knowing, but it is obvious that the more varieties and the more skills we have, the better off we will be."

So, the problem comes out in genetics. We do not really know how to interfere with the way things are. The world actually is an enormously complex interrelated organism. The same problem arises in medicine because the body, too, is a very complexly interrelated organism. If you look at the body in a superficial way you may see there is something wrong with it and end up only treating the outward manifestation rather than the cause. Let us say you have chicken pox, the cause of which is something in the blood; it is some kind of a bug and it comes out in itchy spots all over the body. But you do not want to cut off the spots; what you have to do is kill the bug. So you kill the bug. Well, then you find you have real problems because you have to introduce other bugs to kill that bug. It is like bringing rabbits into Australia, everything gets out of hand. So you think, "Well, now wait a minute. It was not just the bugs in the blood; there are bugs all over the place. The problem with chicken pox is that the blood system suddenly becomes vulnerable to those particular bugs. It must have been that my resistance was down. What I should have taken was not antibiotics but vitamins." Okay, so you are going to build up your resistance, but resistance to what? You may build up resistance to all these types of bugs, but then there is another type that just loves that situation and moves right in. Medically, we always look at the human being in bits and pieces—we have heart specialists, lung specialists, bone specialists, nerve specialists, et cetera—and they each see the human being from their own point of view. There are a few general practitioners, but they realize that the human body is so complicated that no one mind can understand it. Furthermore, supposing we do succeed in healing all these people of their diseases, then what do we do about the population problem? We have stopped cholera, the bubonic plague, we are getting the better of tuberculosis, and we may even fix cancer and heart disease. Then what will people die of? Well, they will just go on living. There will be enormous quantities of us, and so we will have to fix the problem of birth control—pills for everyone. But what about the side effects of those pills, and the psychological effects upon men and women who do not breed children in the usual way? What are they going to do? Are they going to become homosexuals? We do not know. What seems a good thing today, or yesterday, like DDT, turns out tomorrow to have been a disaster. What seemed, in the moral or spiritual sphere, like great virtues in times past, are easily seen today as hideous evils.

Take, for example, the Inquisition. In its own day, among Catholics, the Holy Inquisition was regarded as we today regard the practice of psychiatry. A heretic was a very sick man. He was much to be pitied because if he held a false view he was doomed to suffer forever in the most exquisite torture chamber ever imagined. Think of entertaining that idea as seriously as we regard cancer or schizophrenia today. We feel that in curing a person of disease almost anything is justified: the most complex operations; people suspended for days on the end of tubes with x-ray penetration burning of diseased tissue with lasers; people undergoing shock treatment; people locked in the colorless, monotonous corridors of mental institutions not knowing if they will ever get out because they cannot understand what is expected of them, and the psychiatrists do not know either. It is a kind of Kafka-like nightmare. We think these surgeons and psychiatrists are very good people, that they are righteous men working to alleviate human suffering. Well, they thought exactly the same thing about the Inquisitors. In all good faith, they knew that witchcraft and heresy were terrible things, awful plagues imperiling people's souls forever. Any means were justified to cure people of heresy; and we have not changed. We are doing the same thing today but under different names. We can look back at those people and see how evil that was, but we cannot see it in ourselves.

So beware of virtue! The Chinese philosopher, Lao-tzu, said that the highest virtue is not conscious of itself as virtue, and therefore really is virtue; but lower virtue is so self-conscious of itself as virtue that it is not virtue. In other words, when you breathe, you do not congratulate yourself on being virtuous, but breathing is a great virtue; it is living. When you are born with beautiful eyes, blue, brown, or green, as the case may be, you do not congratulate yourself for having grown two of the most fabulous jewels on earth. You say, "Oh, they are just eyes." But do you not account it a virtue to see, to entertain the miracles of color and form? You say, "Well, that is just seeing." But that is real virtue. Real virtue, in the old sense of the word, infers strength, as when you speak of the healing virtue of a plant. The other virtues are just stuck on, they are imitation virtues, and they usually create trouble. More diabolical things are done in the name of righteousness, and you can be assured that everyone, of whatever nationality or political frame of mind or religion, always goes to war with a sense of complete rightness—the other side is the devil. Our opponents, whether in China, Russia, or Vietnam, have the same feeling of righteousness about what they are doing as we have on our side. And "a plague on both houses!" As Confucius said, "The goody-goodies are the thieves of virtue," which is another form of our own proverb, "The road to hell is paved with good intentions."

So the moral, or the immoral, of these considerations is that if you are really aware of your own inner workings, you will realize that there is nothing you can do to improve yourself. You do not even know what "better" is, and, in any case, the you who will do the improving is the one who needs to be improved. This also goes for society.

We can change society. We can get enormously enthusiastic about the idea that there is a revolution afoot, and that it will set everything to right. But do you know a revolution that has ever set everything to right? It does not matter whether the revolution came from the left wing or from the right wing. The best forms of government that have ever existed in the world are those that muddled through, those that did not have any clear setup of control. They had what I would call "controlled anarchy," and this system seems to work out better than anything else. When you have a great system and real power to put it into effect there is always more violence, more bloodshed, more trouble. It makes no difference whether it be Chairman Mao or Adolf Hitler. We cannot outwit ourselves, we cannot be unself-conscious on purpose, we cannot be designedly spontaneous, and we cannot be genuinely loving by intending to love. Either you love someone or you do not. If you pretend to love a person, you deceive them and build up reasons for resentment. Today we hear a lot of songs about love, and the mention of the big love thing on the way. You know what I would do? I would buy a gun and bar my door because I would know there is a storm of hypocrisy brewing. You know, a bunch of little buggers come around and say, "Well, you should not mind our taking your stuff; after all, nothing really belongs to anybody and surely you are a loving and spiritual person and want to share everything."

Let us look at this from another point of view, one that you will at first think highly depressing. Let us suppose that we cannot do anything to change ourselves. Suppose we are stuck with it. Now that is the worst thing an American audience can hear—there is no way of improving yourselves. Every kind of culture in this country is dedicated to self-improvement. Why do some people go to the opera or the symphony? Only a small fraction of the audience goes to the symphony to enjoy it. The rest go to be seen there and to see themselves there because that is culture, that is doing what is good for you. Take jogging, that deplorable practice. It is a very nice thing to run and go dancing across the hills at a fast speed, but we see these joggers shaking their bones, rattling their brains, and running on their heels. There is a grimness about it because it is so determinately good for you. Why do you go to school? There is only one reason for going to school, and that is because someone there has something that you want to find out. The whole point of going to school is that you are interested in something. You do not go to improve yourself, but the trouble is that the schools have the wrong idea—they give people honors for learning. The reward for studying French should be the ability to speak French, to enjoy reading French, and to have fun with French people. But when you get a degree for it, then the degree becomes the point in a game of one-upmanship.

Of course, one-upmanship is the main business of the educational community today. You learn all the rules of how to be a good professor. It is very instructive to go to a professor's meeting. In my field, which is philosophy, you go to a congress of philosophers and you find that when they all get together in the bar or the restaurant, or in someone's room, the one thing they never talk about is philosophy. It is very bad form, indeed, to show interest in philosophy among your colleagues. The same is exactly true in clergy gatherings. The one thing they do not talk about is religion. What they both do talk about is church and academic politics. You see, it is bad form to be brilliant on the faculty because if outclasses your colleagues. Therefore, faculty people tend to cultivate a studied mediocrity. You have to watch out because if you have mobs of students coming to your lectures, you get pretty black looks from your colleagues. Then, of course, there is a whole world of one-upmanship in research and publication, of learned papers and the relative quantity of footnotes to basic text, and footnotes on footnotes, and the various ways of making your bibliography painfully accurate. It is endless. But you see, what it is, it is scholarship about scholarship. Just as learning because learning is good for you is irrelevant to learning, the whole idea of improving yourself by learning is irrelevant to the learning process. In the same way, doing business is doing business. Being a manufacturer of clothing is a very good thing to do. I could conceive that it would be extremely enjoyable, something one could be very proud of, to make good clothes. Of course, you would need to sell them because you need to eat. But to make clothes to make money raises another question, because then your interest is not in making clothes, it is in making money, and then you are going to cheat on the clothes. Suppose you get an awful lot of money, then what would you do with it? You cannot eat ten roasts of beef in one day. You cannot live in six houses at once. You cannot drive three Rolls Royces at the same time. What could you do? Well, you could just go make more money and put it back, you could invest it in something else so that it would make more, and not give a damn how it is made so long as you make it. You do not care if they foul the rivers, put oil fumes throughout the air everywhere, and kill off all the fish. So long as you see these figures happening, you are not aware of anything else.

So you went out to do a self-improvement thing—making money is a measure of improvement, a measure of your economic worth, or at least that is what it is supposed to be—but you went out, in other words, for the status instead of the actuality. If you are a musician, why do you play music? The only reason for playing music is to enjoy it. If you play music to imrpess an audience or to read about yourself in the newspaper, then you are not interested in music.

Here is the situation: the whole idea of self-improvement is a will-o'-the-wisp and a hoax. Let us begin where we are. What happens if you know beyond any shadow of a doubt that there is nothing that you can do to be better? Well, it is a kind of relief. I am what I am, there it is. So you say, "Now what will I do?", and there is a little fidget that comes up because we are so used to making things better— "leave the world a little better than when you found it" sort of thing, or "I want to be of service to other people," and all such dreadfully hazy ideas. There is that little itch still. But if we realize that there really is nothing we can do to improve ourselves or to improve the world, it gives us a breather in the course of which we may simply watch what is happening. No one ever does this. It sounds terribly simple, it sounds so simple that it looks almost as if it is not worth doing. But have you ever just watched what is happening, and what you are doing by way of reaction to it? Just watch it happen, and do not be in a hurry to think you know what it is. People look and say, "Well, that is the external world." How do you know? The whole thing, from a neurological point of view, is just a happening in your head. That you think there is something outside the skull is a notion in your nervous system. There may or may not be. That this is the material world, is someone's philosophical idea. Or maybe you think the world is spiritual; that, too, is someone's philosophical idea. The real world is not spiritual, it is not material, the real world is simply *as it is*.

Do you think we could look at things in this way, without, as it were, fixing labels, names, gradations, and judgments on everything? Could we just watch what happens, watch what we do? If you do that, you do at least give yourself a chance. And it may be that when you are in this way freed from being out to improve everything, that your own nature will begin to take care of itself. Once you get out of your own way, you will begin to find out that the great things that you do are really happenings. No great genius can explain how he does it. He says, "Yes, I have learned a technique to express myself because I had something in me that had to come out. I had to learn how to give it." If you are a musician you have to learn how music is produced, or if you want to describe something you have to learn a language so that others can understand you. You need a technique. But beyond that, can you tell someone how you were able to use that technique to express the mysterious thing that you wanted to tell them? If we could tell people that, we would have schools in which we could infallibly train musical geniuses and scientific miracle minds. There would be so many of them that geniuses would be a dime a dozen. Then we would say, "Well, these people are not very ingenious after all." The fascinating element about genius is that it produces something we cannot understand, it surprises us. But do you not see that, just in the same way, we cannot even understand our own brains, which is only to say that the brain is a lot smarter that neurology. Our brain is such that it can perform all these extraordinary intellectual and cultural miracles; we do not know *how* we do it, but we do. We did not campaign to have an improved brain over the monkeys, or whatever may have been our ancestors; it just happened.

All growth is fundamentally something that happens, but for it to happen, two things are important. The first is, as I have said, you must have the technical ability to express what happens; and secondly, you must get out of your own way. But right at the bottom of the problem of control is "How am I to get out of my own way?" If I showed you a system—"Let's all practice getting out of our own way" —it would only turn into another form of self-improvement. We find this problem repeatedly throughout the entire history of human spirituality. In the phraseology of Zen Buddhism, "You cannot achieve this by thinking, you cannot achieve this by not thinking." Getting out of your own way comes about only when doing so ceases to be a matter of choice, because you see that there is nothing else for you to do. In other words, it happens when you see that doing something about your situation is not going to help you, and that trying *not* to do anything about it is equally not going to help you. Then where do you stand? You are nonplussed. You are simply reduced to watching, and letting it be.

CHAPTER FIVE

CHUANG-TZU

Wisdom of the Ridiculous

THE CHINESE philosopher, Chuang-tzu, who lived about 300 B.C., or perhaps even a little earlier, was a very remarkable person. He is one of the only philosophers from the whole of antiquity who has any real humor, and therefore, he is an immensely encouraging person to read.

Part of Chuang-tzu's humor is in the art of exaggeration, which is something I think we must always allow for. So in reading his work we must realize that he is pulling his own leg to some extent. He is like a group of enthusiasts who, when talking amongst themselves, carry their own ideas to ludicrous extremes and roar with laughter about them. Chuang-tzu does this, but in doing so he has a lot to say about the value of the useless life.

The whole notion that any event in life might be useful, that is to say, serving the end of some future event, is to a Taoist absurd. The universe is viewed as purposeless and useless through and through. It is a game, and yet it is more than that, because to call it a game does not really convey the sense of it. For example, when a Taoist sage is wandering through the forest, he is not going anywhere, he is just wandering. When he watches the clouds, he loves them because they have no special destination. He watches birds flying, and he watches waves slapping on the shore. Just because all this is not busy in the way that human beings are normally busy, and because it serves no end other than being what it is now, he admires it. It is for this reason that you get the peculiar styles of Chinese painting in the T'ang, Sung, and later dynasties, where nature in its aimless, wandering way is the main subject of interest. Usually, when we say that something is without purpose, that is a put-down phrase. We say, "Well, there is no future in it. What is the use?" It is funny that we say, "What is the use?", and I think we should realize that this question reflects our insanity. The joy for the Taoist is that things have no use, and the future is not important.

Now, one can exaggerate this, and Chuang-tzu does so in a very humorous way when he describes the ideal, useless man. This man is a hunchback who is so deformed that his chin rests on his navel, and yet he is very admirable because it appears to everyone else that he has found the secret to life. When the social service workers come around, he is the first to get a free handout, and when the military officers come around to conscript people for the army he is the first to be rejected. Therefore, he lives a long life.

Chuang-tzu tells another story in which he describes a group of travelers who came across an enormous tree. Never had anyone seen such a fantastic tree, so they went up to see if it might be useful for some purpose. First they tested the leaves, but found them too rough and disagreeable and not good to eat. Then they looked at the branches and found them all twisted and absolutely no good for using as sticks; so then they examined the wood, but found it was full of pith and absolutely no good to use in building. As a result, no one ever disturbed this tree. It was not useful for any purpose whatsoever, and so it had grown to an enormous size and was of great age. Chuang-tzu is not exactly asking us to take this literally, but this is his way of doing things.

In another story he describes the behavior of the highest form of man:

> The man of character lives at home without exercising his mind and performs actions without worry. The notions of right and wrong and the praise and blame of others do not disturb him. When within the four seas all people can enjoy themselves, that is happiness for him. When all people are well-provided, that is peace for him. Sorrowful in countenance, he looks like a baby who has lost his mother; appearing stupid, he goes about like one who has lost his way. He has plenty of money to spend, but does not know where it comes from. He drinks and eats just enough and does not know where the food comes from. This is the demeanor of the man of character.

Then, by contrast:

> The hypocrites are those people who regard as good whatever the world acclaims as good, and regard as right whatever the world acclaims as right. When you tell them that they are men of Tao, then their countenances change with satisfaction. When you call them hypocrites, then they look displeased. All their lives they call themselves "men of Tao," and all their lives they remain hypocrites. They know how to give a good speech and tell appropriate anecdotes to attract a good crowd. But from the very beginning to the very end, they do not know what it is all about. They put on the proper garb, and dress in the proper colors. They put on a decorous appearance in order to make

themselves popular, but refuse to admit that they are hypocrites.[1]

This explanation of man who is stupid in countenance and appearance, and is wandering about as if he has lost his way and does not know anything, is based on the text of Lao-tzu, where he says:

> The people of the world are merrymaking,
>> As if partaking of the sacrificial feasts,
>> As if mounting the terrace in spring;
> I alone am mild, like one unemployed,
>> Like a new-born babe that cannot yet smile,
>> Unattached, like one without a home.
>
> The people of the world have enough and
>> to spare,
> But I am like one left out,
>> My heart must be that of a fool,
>> Being muddled, nebulous!
>
> The vulgar are knowing, luminous;
>> I alone am dull, confused.
> The vulgar are clever, self-assured;
>> I alone, depressed.
> Patient as the sea,
>> Adrift, seemingly aimless.
>
> The people of the world all have a purpose;
>> I alone appear stubborn and uncouth.
> I alone differ from the other people,
>> And value drawing sustenance from the
>> Mother.[2]

There is about the character of the Taoist sage, as depicted by Chuang-tzu, something of the fool. The fool is a person who does not know enough to come in out of the rain, and who does not compete. Everyone else gets to the material prizes of life before him, and even to the spiritual prizes. The fool is the person who is not going anywhere, He sits by the side of the road talking nonsense. The fool is like a Mongoloid child who is not interested in survival, and who will take a plate of food and run his finger around in it, make a wonderful slosh with the stew, and then watch it drip from the tip of his finger. He will not eat it for quite a while, and then he will play with it in all sorts of ways until his attention is distracted by something else, and he will chase after that. So long as you do not cross him he remains the most wonderfully friendly sort of person, but he does not have any kind of ambition; he does not fight for himself, and nobody can ever get him to.

One might understand why the fool has always been used as a kind of analog of the sage, when, as Shankara says:

> Sometimes naked, sometimes mad,
> Now as a scholar, now as a fool.
> Thus, they appear on earth,
>   the free men.

The biographies of the early life of Sri Ramakrishna, or Sri Ramana reflect this type of understanding, and they are absolutely wild. But, just as in reading Chuang-tzu, you must not take them too literally. These things are said by way of a kind of overstress to correct another kind of overstress in the opposite direction.

Many years ago when a Japanese scholar explained the teaching of Buddhism to me, he said something I have never heard anyone else say since. He said that the Buddha taught that life is suffering in order to correct the wrong view that it ought to be pleasure. He said that everything is impermanent in order to correct the wrong view that reality lasts forever in time. The idea of the middle way is set up in this fashion—of going to one extreme to correct the other. This is a very common Asian technique, and it is found especially in Zen. For example, when teachers are asked about something sacred they will always answer in terms of something secular. When asked, "What is the Buddha?", they might answer, "The tree in the garden." Then, when you ask about something secular, they answer in terms of something sacred. For example, a master and his student were working in the field, using a knife to prune. The student suddenly said to the master, "Give me the knife." So the master gave it to him point first. Then the student said, "Please, let me have the other end," and the teacher said, "What will you do with the other end?" You see, the questions immediately turn into a kind of metaphysical exhange; and this play, back and forth between the extremes, the interior design of awakening the mind to polarity, to mutual arising.

Chuang-tzu's philosophy is one of relativity. He thoroughly stresses the point that there is no absolute standard of great or small, of important or unimportant. He tells a story about a certain keeper of monkeys who said with regard to their ration of nuts that each monkey should have three in the morning and four at night. But at this the monkeys were very angry. So the keeper said they might have four in the morning and three at night, with which arrangement they were all pleased. Now, the number of nuts was the same, he goes on to say, but there was an adaptation to the likes and dislikes of those concerned. This, he says, is the way of conduct of the sage. With Chuang-tzu you begin to get the point of view that small things are as big as big things can be, and that big things are as small as small things can be. Everything can be looked at as great and small, important and unimportant, as well as all the steps in between. His conception of the world is essentially cyclic.

Teaching by circles is a method often used by Taoist and Zen teachers. The center of a circle is understood as any point on the circumference, and you can begin anywhere. There is a Zen koan which asks the question: "Indra built the seamless tower; where did he start?" Now, a seamless tower is like a sleeve without a seam in it, it is a continuous cylindrical tower. Where do you start? In the same way, where does the circle start? The circle of life, or the cycle of life; the interdependence of bees and flowers, and the interdependence of long and short—it is all circular. There is nowhere, and there is everywhere, that it can begin. When Chuang-tzu discusses the organs of the body he makes a catalog of all these organs, and says, "Now, which do you prefer? Which one comes first, and which one follows? Which one rules, and which ones are servants?" It semeed that there might be a governor in all this, but nobody could ever find it. Thus, there is no notion in Taoist philosophy— one might almost say in Chinese philosophy as a whole— of the world as responding to a boss. Within the body there is no ruling organ; its order is the consequence of, or the operation of, every part of it existing together, simultaneously, arising mutually. There is no governor. Now, the difficulty which arises in trying to understand Chuang-tzu's philosophy is that people begin to think in terms of governing and ruling, and they set out to dominate themselves and their surroundings, which invariably leads to a mess. Chuang-tzu tells a story of an ancient man by the name of Po Loh. Po Loh was a horse trainer, and this is perhaps where we get the word "polo." Chuang-tzu says that horses were nice, charming creatures before Po Loh interfered with them and ruined their nature. In other places he says that a good carpenter does not need a square or a compass; he works without them. This is fantastically true of Japanese carpenters. One of the fascinating things in going to Japan is watching these old-style carpenters working from the roughest architectural plans you could imagine. They use the strangest instruments, and have an uncanny knack for fitting things by feel and by eye.

A great story is told of the ceremonial raising of the ridgepole of a new temple. It was being done by a certain guild of carpenters, but there was a rival guild in town that had not got the contract, and was very sore about it. So during the night one of the members of the rival guild came and chopped off six feet or so of the ridgepole. When the master craftsman came in the morning, and all the priests had arrived for the ceremony of raising the roof beam, he looked at it and said, "Somebody has interfered with this. It must have been our enemy guild. They have cut off six feet of the ridgepole. Oh well," he said, "I will put it right." So he took his hammer and ceremonially struck the beam, then said, "Raise it." It was raised and it fit exactly. The story is, of course, that he knew that this would happen and so he made the beam too long. This sort of story is always associated with the carpenter's art. He needs no square because the sense of skill that is in his organism, in his nerves, in his senses, is much more subtle than anything that could be made with instruments.

There are many stories about artists of the Far East who excel in this kind of thing—knowing with tremendous precision exactly where something should go. There is a story told about a master who was decorating a ceremonial tea room with his students, when one of the students asked him where to put a hook for hanging a bamboo vase for flowers on the wall. The master said with exactness, "There." So the student made a little mark. Well, somewhat later, the student intentionally rubbed out the mark, but he remembered where it should go by a tiny little prick in the wall. Then he said to the teacher, "Excuse me, sir, but I forgot where you said the vase should go." The teacher said, "It was there," and he put his finger exactly on the same spot as before. This is the sort of thing that is admired by students in the Far East.

The whole principle which Chuang-tzu explains at great length is one of success in life through not pushing it around, through not trying to govern it. For example, he explains that music has been ruined by the five notes. He says:

> The five notes will make a man deaf;
> The five colors will make a man blind.

What he means by this is that if you think there are only five notes, you cannot hear, and if you think there are only five colors, you cannot see. This is a problem we have with music in the West. We have a notation system that indicates our chromatic scale and the staff, and the way we write music is limited to that possibility. But there are all kinds of subtleties between every one of our notes. In writing our rhythm we have to go in steps from whole note, half note, quarter note, eighth note, sixteenth note, and so on; and we can increase the value by one half by dotting it. But that is the extent of our rhythmic expression. In Oriental music they have an infinite continuum of rhythm and tone, and so they make the most extraordinarily complicated rhythms. The way they learn music is not from notation, or from measures, but from the living body of their teacher as he demonstrates the ways of playing a certain instrument. They follow the teacher, the man, instead of the words and symbols.

There is an absolutely absurd translation of Chuang-tzu put out by a professor of Chinese at Harvard. I am sure this professor must be an ex-missionary because he keeps using the word "God," when there is no expression in the *Chuang-tzu* for God. The notion of God as we understand it is, indeed, very foreign to Taoist thought. The missionaries, you must understand, have been the foundation of Chinese scholarship in the West. In order to translate the scriptures into English, they had to study Chinese, and they have been slipping Christian ideas into Chinese classics ever since. But the notion of God, in the sense of the personal ruler of the world, is totally foreign to Chinese thought. There is the expression *ch'ien-jan* which has almost the same meaning as *tzu-jan*—spontaneity, or "self-so-ness." *Ch'ien-jan* refers to something that is so through the power of heaven. Heaven, or *ch'ien*, means simply the universe. As you look out from Earth, which is, as it were, the center or the base, everything else in the whole expanse of the cosmos is *ch'ien*, heaven. But in Chuang-tzu, there is no connection in the idea of heaven with some sort of personal ruler of the universe. When you see someone translating *ch'ien* as "God," it gives a very wrong impression of this teaching.

There is a passage in which a student asks the master, "Can one get the Tao so as to have it for one's own?" And the sage answers, "Your body is not your own, it is the delegated image of *ch'ien*." The missionaries translate this as "God" because they have read in the Bible that man is made in the image of God. But the master says:

> Your life is not your own, it is the delegated adaptability of heaven. Your offspring are not your own, they are the delegated seeds of heaven. You move, you know not how; you are at rest, you know not why. These are the operations of the ways of Tao.

So how could you get the Tao so as to have it for your own?

Similarly, there is a passage which says that when a drunk man falls out of a cart, though he may suffer, he does not die. Because his spirit is in a condition of security, he does not suffer from contact with objects of existences. If such security may be got from wine, how much more from *ch'ien-jan*?

What is revealed here is the effortlessness of being in accord with the spontaneous rhythm of the universe. In Chinese thought there is not even an idea for what we call the law of nature. The motions of the body and the harmony of the organism are not what they are because of any obedience to a law. The Chinese do have an idea of law which is expressed by the word *tzu*. There was a time when the laws were inscribed on the sacrificial vessels so that when people came to offer their sacrifices they would read the laws. Certain sages objected to this and said that if the people were expected to know what the laws were in the fixed terms of writing they would develop a literary spirit. That is to say, they would start haggling about what it really said. Well, as you know, this is the principle occupation of lawyers. But the point that the Taoist sages were making is that you must not write it down like that. They describe the Tao as *wu-tzu*, which we would translate literally as "lawless"; but what it means is the transcending of this kind of law, which is specific or positive law.

In continuing to explain this principle of lawlessness, Chuang-tzu employs a very funny little trick. He often puts his own wisdom into the mouth of Confucius, and this is to the immense confusion of everyone else. He tells us that one day Confucius was standing by a river near where there was a tremendous cataract plunging down. Suddenly he saw an old man coming out of the forest who fell into the river and disappeared into the cataract. So he said, "Oh, dear, too bad. Probably some old fellow tired of life wanted to put an end to it all." But in the next moment, way down the stream, the old man gets out of the water and starts bouncing along. Confucius is amazed! He sends one of his disciples to catch this fellow before he disappears. On meeting him he says, "Sir, I was thinking that you were going to commit suicide and I suddenly find that you have come out of that cataract alive. Do you have some special method by which you did this?" "No, I have no special method," said the old man, "I just go in with a whirl and come out with a swirl. I do not resist the water, I entirely identify myself with it." So here is this old man, utterly relaxed, rolling around in the current and not resisting in any way, and so he is preserved. He goes with the stream and he rolls with the punch.

Again, of course, there is exaggeration in a story of this

kind, because true *wu-wei,* or letting go, noninterference, is an exaggeration stressing the yin point of view to compensate for the yang. Relaxation is simply something that happens when there is too much yang in you—too much of the active principle that needs to be balanced out by the passive, or yin principle. The trouble is that human beings in their anxiety to control things exhibit too much yang aggressiveness; and yet, in balancing this out with the yin principle of letting go, one must not confuse it with, for example, flabbiness. A lot of people when they are trying to relax, merely become flabby. Furthermore, there is the obvious difficulty that if, in trying to relax, you feel you must relax, you only get anxious and create further tension in the process. I remember reading a book called *You Must Relax.* Now, you cannot achieve *wu-wei* like that. Even in trying to relax you are tense; you are anxious that it must happen, and afraid that it will not. Then how on earth do you do it? First of all you have to understand that you do not have to do anything. As the Old Man said, there is no method. Taoists use the term *wu-tzu,* lawlessness, to mean that there is no method that you can master to do it. It is all based on the understanding, or what our psychologists call insight, that there is nothing that you can do as a source and cause of action separate from everything else. When you know that, that there is no separate-acting you, then there is no need to try to relax. The flow of the Tao goes on. You can try and swim against the river if you wish, but it really is much easier to go with it. Just like the flow of time—you cannot get out of the present moment. You can think about the past and you can think about the future, but since you do that thinking now, the present is inescapable. All right, now the present moment does, does it not, have a sense of flow. Time is going along; life is going along. Clock time is simply a measure of flow, a way of going tick, tick, tick, tick, and counting the ticks. Well, we have lived through so many ticks, but nevertheless, real time, as distinct from ticking, is a flowing; yet, it is still. Is it not fascinating that it moves, but you are always there; it is always now. You never get out of now.

This is the principle of flowing. It is beautifully simple. But you can think of all kinds of very clever ways to postpone finding this out. You can say, "Well, this is a very spiritual matter, and I am an unevolved person, so it will take me a very long time to realize this in more than an intellectual way." But this is just an excuse for playing your own game, and not finding this out. There are all sorts of elaborate ways of doing this, and you can put it off by indulging in the most complicated systems of spiritual culture, or yoga, and so on, and so forth. And that is all right, I have no objection to your putting it off if that is what you want to do. But actually, it is always here and now. Just as you cannot get away from now, you cannot get out of the Tao. That is the humor of the whole thing, and that is why Chuang-tzu has this beautiful light touch. He says:

> The heron is white without a daily bath.
> The crow is black without being painted
>   in ink.

Therefore, there are blondes and brunettes, fat people and skinny people, tall people and short people, cultured people and vulgar people. Even the Christian hymn says:

> The rich man in his castle,
>   the poor man at his gate,
> God made them high and lowly,
>   and ordered their estate.

Of course, we do not sing that much now, because we have too much social conscience.

Chuang-tzu has this to say about that:

> Those who say that they would have right without
> its correlate wrong, or good government without its

correlate misrule, do not apprehend the great principle of the universe, nor the nature of all creation. One might as well talk of the existence of heaven without earth, or of the negative principle, yin, without the positive, yang; which is clearly impossible. If people keep on discussing it without stop, such people must be either fools or knaves.

Of course, one could always reply to Chuang-tzu that there have to be fools and knaves so that we can recognize the existence of sages! He says as much in another way here:

Speech is not mere blowing of breath, it is intended to say something, only what it is intended to say cannot yet be determined. Is there speech indeed, or is there not? Can we, or can we not, distinguish it from the chirping of young birds?

How can Tao be so obscured that there can be a distinction of true and false? How can speech be so obscured that there can be a distinction of right and wrong? Where can you go and find Tao not to exist? Where can you go and find that words cannot be proved? The Tao is obscured by our inadequate understanding, and words are obscured by flowery expressions. Hence, the affirmations and denials of the Confucian and the Mohian schools, each denying what the other affirms and affirming what the other denies. Each denying what the other affirms and affirming what the other denies brings us only confusion.

There is nothing which is not this, there is nothing which is not that. What cannot be seen by "that" (the other person) can be known by myself; hence, I say, "this" emanates from "that"; "that" also derives from "this." This is the theory of the interdependence of "this" and "that." Nevertheless, life arises from death and vice versa. Possibility arises from impossibility, and vice versa. Affirmation is based upon denial, and vice versa. Which being the case, the true sage rejects all distinctions and takes refuge in heaven.

For one may base it on this, yet this is also that, and that is also this. This also has its right and wrong, and that has its right and wrong; does then, the distinction between this and that really exist or not? When this, the subjective, and that, the objective, are both without their correlates, that is the very axis of Tao. And when that axis passes through the center at which all infinities converge, affirmations and denials alike blend into the Infinite One. Hence, it is said that there is nothing like using the Light.

You see, the axis of the opposites is the perception of their polarity. The difference between them is explicit, but the unity of them is implicit. There is the explicit difference between two ends of a stick, and the implicit unity that they are ends of the same stick. This is what is understood as the axis. The axis of Tao is what you might call the "secret conspiracy" that lies between all poles and opposites. It is implicit, or esoteric, that they are fundamentally one. Unity, whether it is between you and the universe, or any polarity, is not something that has to be brought into being. If one brings it into being one assumes that it does not exist, and this is called in Zen, putting "legs on a snake" or "a beard on a eunuch"—it is just unnecessary. Unity exists; it is always there. You can see it so vividly, and actually *almost* put your finger on it and sense it. But, of course, if you try to grab the present moment and say, "Get ready, get ready, NOW!"—it is gone! The finer and finer we draw the hairline on the watch to know exactly when *now* is, the closer we eventually get to where we cannot see it at all. But, if you leave it alone and do not try to grab the moment as it flies, it is always there. You do not have to mark it, you do not have to put your finger on it, because it is everything that there is. And so, the present moment suddenly expands. It contains the whole of time, all past, all future, everything. You never have to hold on to it. If you can feel that, then realize that the movement of the Tao is exactly the same thing as the present moment—that which we call *now* is the same thing as the Tao. The Tao, the course of things, the eternal now, the presence of God, anything you want to call it— that is *now*! And you cannot get out of it. There is no need to get with it because you cannot get away from it! That is beautiful. You just relax, and you are there.

THE PRACTICE OF
MEDITATION

The practice of meditation is not what is ordinarily meant by practice, in the sense of repetitious preparation for some future performance. It may seem odd and illogical to say that meditation in the form of yoga, Dhyana, or Za-zen, as used by Hindus and Buddhists, is a practice without purpose – in some future time – because it is the art of being completely centered in the here and now. "I'm not sleepy, and there is no place I'm going to."

We are living in a culture entirely hypnotized by the illusion of time, in which the so-called present moment is felt as nothing but an infinitesimal hairline between an all-powerfully causative past and an absorbingly important future. We have no present. Our consciousness is almost completely preoccupied with memory and expectation. We do not realize that there never was, is, or will be any other experience than present experience.

We are therefore out of touch with reality. We confuse the world as talked about, described, and measured with the world which actually is. We are sick with a fascination for the useful tools of names and numbers, of symbols, signs, conceptions, and ideas. Meditation is therefore the art of suspending verbal and symbolic thinking for a time, somewhat as a courteous audience will stop talking when a concert is about to begin.

Simply sit down, close your eyes, and listen to all sounds that may be going on—without trying to name or identify them. Listen as you would listen to music. If you find that verbal thinking will not drop away, don't attempt to stop it by force of will-power. Just keep your tongue relaxed, floating easily in the lower jaw, and listen to your thoughts as if they were birds chattering outside—mere noise in the skull—and they will eventually subside of themselves, as a turbulent and muddy pool will become calm and clear if left alone.

Also, become aware of breathing and allow your lungs to work in whatever rhythm seems congenial to them. And for a while just sit listening and feeling breath. But, if possible, don't call it that. Simply experience the non-verbal happening. You may object that this is not "spiritual" meditation but mere attention to the "physical" world, but it should be understood that the spiritual and the physical are only ideas, philosophical conceptions, and that the reality of which you are now aware is not an idea. Furthermore, there is no "you" aware of it. That was also just an idea. Can you hear yourself listening?

And then begin to let your breath "fall" out, slowly and easily. Don't force or strain your lungs, but let the breath come out in the same way that you let yourself slump into a comfortable bed. Simply let

it go, go, and go. As soon as there is the least
strain, just let it come back in as a reflex; don't
pull it in. Forget the clock. Forget to count. Just
keep it up for so long as you feel the luxury of it.

Using the breath in this way, you discover how to
generate energy without force. For example, one of
the gimmicks {in Sanskrit, upaya} used to quiet
the thinking mind and its compulsive chattering is
known as mantra — the chanting of sounds for the
sake of sound rather than meaning. Therefore begin
to "float" a single tone on the long, easy outbreath
at whatever pitch is most comfortable. Hindus and
Buddhists use for this practice such syllables as
ŌM, AH, HUM {i.e. HUNG}, and Christians might
prefer AMEN or ALLELUIA, Muslims ALLAH, and
Jews ADONAI : it really makes no difference, since
what is important is simply and solely the sound.
Like Zen Buddhists, you could use just the syllable
MŌOO {無}. Dig that, and let your consciousness
sink down, down, down into the sound for as long
as there is no sense of strain.

Above all, don't look for a result, for some
marvellous change of consciousness or satori: the
whole essence of meditation-practice is centering
upon what IS — not on what should or might be.
The point is not to make the mind blank or to
concentrate fiercely upon, say, a single point of light —
although that, too, can be delightful without the
fierceness.

For how long should this be kept up? My own, and
perhaps unorthodox, feeling is that it can be continued
for as long as there is no sensation of forcing it —
and this may easily extend to 30 or 40 minutes at
one sitting, whereafter you will want to return to

the state of normal restlessness and distraction.

In sitting for meditation, it is best to use a substantial cushion on the floor, to keep the spine erect but not stiff, to have the hands on the lap—palms upwards—resting easily upon each other, and to sit cross-legged like a Buddha-figure, either in full or half "lotus" posture, or kneeling and sitting back on the heels. "Lotus" means placing one or both feet sole upwards upon the opposite thigh. These postures are slightly uncomfortable, but they have, therefore, the advantage of keeping you awake!

In the course of meditation you may possibly have astonishing visions, amazing ideas, and fascinating fantasies. You may also feel that you are becoming clairvoyant or that you are able to leave your body and travel at will. But all that is distraction. Leave it alone and simply watch what happens NOW. One does not meditate in order to acquire extraordinary powers, for if you managed to become omnipotent and omniscient, what would you do? There would be no further surprises for you, and your whole life would be like making love to a plastic woman. Beware, then, of all those gurus who promise "marvellous results" and other future benefits from their disciplines. The whole point is to realize that there is no future, and that the real sense of life is an exploration of the eternal now. STOP, LOOK, and LISTEN! Or shall we say, "Turn on, tune in, and drop in"?

A story is told of a man who came to the Buddha with offerings of flowers in both hands. The Buddha said, "Drop it!" So he dropped the flowers in his left hand. The Buddha said again "Drop it!" He dropped the flowers in his right hand. And the Buddha said, "Drop that which you have neither in the right nor in the left, but in the middle!" And the man was instantly enlightened.

It is marvellous to have the sense that all living and moving is dropping, or going along with gravity. After all—the earth is falling around the sun, and, in turn, the sun is falling around some other star. For energy is precisely a taking of the line of least resistance. Energy is mass. The power of water is in following its own weight. All comes to him who weights.

NOTES

FOREWORD

1. Alan Watts, *This Is It* (New York: Vintage Books, 1973), pp. 19, 21.

2. Mircea Eliade, *The Two and the One* (New York: Harper & Row, 1952), p. 77.

3. Watts, op. cit., pp. 30–31.

4. K. C. Varadachari, *Alvars of South India* (Bombay: Bharatiya Vidya Bhavan, 1970), p. 178.

CHAPTER ONE

1. *Zoku-Kosoden* (Ch., *Hsu Kao-seng Chuan*).

2. *Mumonkan* (Ch., *Wu-men Kuan*), case 19.

3. In Chinese, *wu* (no, nothing).

4. In Chinese, *kung-an* (public case).

5. *Kattoshu* (Ch., *Ko-t'eng Chi*).

6. *Rinzai Roku: Shishu* (Ch., *Lin-chi Lu: Shih-chung*).

7. *Bokuju Roku* (Ch., *Mu-chou Lu*).

8. *Zenrin Ruiju,* ch. 2.

9. *Mumonkan,* case 41.

10. *Keitoku Dento Roku* (Ch., *Ching-te ch'uan-teng Lu*), vol. 3.

11. In Chinese, *tzu-jan* (spontaneity or naturalness).

12. *Zenrin Kushu.*

13. *Keitoku Dento Roku,* ch. 8.

14. *Joshu Shinsai Zenji Go Roku* (Ch., *Chao-chou Chen-chi Ch'an-shih Yu-lu*).

15. In Chinese, *wu-hsin* (no-mind, or unself-consciousness) and *wu-nien* (no-thought, or letting go of thoughts and impressions).

16. *Ummon Roku* (Ch., *Yun-men Lu*).

17. Ibid.

18. *Rinzai Roku.*

19. *Goso Roku* (Ch., *Wu-tsu Lu*).

20. In Chinese, *wu-wei* (not-making, or growing naturally).

CHAPTER THREE

1. John 12:24
2. John 16:7
3. Isaiah 45:6–7

CHAPTER FIVE

1. *See* Herbert A. Giles, ed. and trans., *Chuang-tzu: Mystic, Moralist, and Social Reformer* (Shanghai: Kelly and Walsh, 1926) for all references to the *Chuang-tzu.*

2. *See* Lin Yutang, ed. and trans., *The Wisdom of Lao-tse* (New York: Modern Library, 1948).

The "weathermark" identifies this book as a production of John Weatherhill, Inc., publishers of fine books on Asia and the Pacific. Book design and typography by Miriam F. Yamaguchi and Stephen B. Comee. Composition by Samhwa Printing Company, Seoul. Printing by Shōbundō Printing Company, Tokyo. Binding by the Makoto Binderies, Tokyo. The typeface used is Monotype Perpetua.